DONALD TRUMP

REAL ESTATE MOGUL AND PRESIDENT

Published in 2018 by Enslow Publishing, LLC.
101 W. 23rd Street, Suite 240, New York, NY 10011
Copyright © 2018 by Sara McIntosh Wooten

Library of Congress Cataloging-in-Publication Data

Names: Wooten, Sara McIntosh, author.
Title: Donald Trump : real estate mogul and president / Sara McIntosh Wooten.
Description: New York, NY : Enslow Publishing, LLC., 2018. | Series title: Influential lives | Includes bibliographical references and index. | Audience: Grade 6 to 12.
Identifiers: LCCN 2016057796 | ISBN 9780766084995 (library bound : alk. paper)
Subjects: Trump, Donald, 1946-—Juvenile literature. | Businessmen—United States—Biography—Juvenile literature. | Real estate developers—United States—Biography—Juvenile literature. | Celebrities—United States—Biography—Juvenile literature. | Television personalities—United States—Biography—Juvenile literature. | Presidential candidates—United States—Biography—Juvenile literature.
Classification: LCC HC102.5.T78 W663 2017 | DDC 333.33092 B
LC record available at: https://lccn.loc.gov/2016057796

Printed in the United States of America

To Our Readers: We have done our best to make sure all websites in this book were active and appropriate when we went to press. However, the author and the publisher have no control over and assume no liability for the material available on those websites or on any websites they may link to. Any comments or suggestions can be sent by e-mail to customerservice@enslow.com.

Portions of this book originally appeared in the book *Donald Trump: From Real Estate to Reality TV.*

Contents

Republican Roller Coaster

· · · · · · · · · · ·

As hundreds watched and cameras frantically clicked and flashed, Donald Trump and his wife, Melania, slowly and dramatically descended the three-story escalator in Trump Tower to the tower's grand lobby. It was June 16, 2015, and Donald Trump was ready to announce his intent to run for president of the United States. Trump would be joining the race with others, such as Jeb Bush, former governor of Florida, and Ted Cruz, US senator from Texas, along with fourteen other candidates. All were hoping to become the Republican Party nominee for president in the 2016 election.

This was not the first time Trump had flirted with stepping into the political arena. Just four years earlier he had toyed with the idea of running for president against President Barack Obama in the 2012 election.

Donald Trump descended the escalator to the Trump Tower lobby on June 16, 2015, to announce his candidacy for the presidency.

But he ended up bowing out, explaining that he did not want to leave his many business ventures and his popular television show, *Celebrity Apprentice*.[1] By 2015, however, Trump felt he was ready to run. He claimed he was disgusted with how the country was being run, and he wanted to fix it.

A Washington Outsider

From the beginning, Trump's candidacy was considered to be a long shot. Few thought him to be a serious candidate with any real possibility of winning. After all, unlike most of the other Republican candidates, he had no experience in politics.

> He claimed he was disgusted with how the country was being run, and he wanted to fix it.

Trump, however, was not deterred. He saw his status as a Washington outsider to be a huge advantage. He realized that in many elections his lack of political experience might have been a disadvantage. But 2015 was different. Many Americans viewed the government as ineffective and thought that it had not been able to accomplish much of anything over the preceding seven years. With that concern, many saw an advantage to having a totally new face in Washington.

Along with his lack of political experience, Trump also proved he was not a conventional candidate. In his announcement speech, he emphasized his successful business career and experience as a first-rate negotiator.

Trump also mentioned several policy stances he favored. He claimed that creating jobs would be among his top priorities. He took a strong position against undocumented immigration, announcing that if he became president, he would build a formidable wall along the United States border with Mexico. Not only that; he would make Mexico pay for the wall. In addition, he proclaimed that he would fund his campaign with his own money, thereby avoiding any appearance of catering to the interests of would-be donors. His campaign slogan became "Make America Great Again."

With his June 16 declaration, Trump entered the Republican primary process. Over the next several months, he and the other sixteen candidates would hold rallies and campaigns to build voter support and raise money to fund their campaigns. Several debates were televised, giving the general public an opportunity to become familiar with the candidates. All the preparation was designed to build support for the Republican primary elections, which each state would hold, and which would determine the Republican nominee for president.

As Trump campaigned, he continued to garner controversy. He complained about the character of undocumented Latino immigrants, saying they were bringing lots of problems into our country. He made disparaging remarks about women. He attacked John McCain, long-time senator from Arizona, calling him a failed war hero because he had been captured by the enemy. He spoke informally at his rallies, sometimes using inappropriate language. And he complained frequently and bitterly whenever he thought he was being treated

Donald Trump speaks to thousands of listeners at one of his many campaign rallies. He quickly became known as an unconventional candidate, expressing his views simply and bluntly.

• • • • • • • • • • • • • • • • • • • •

unfairly by the media or the Republican Party. He harshly criticized the current government administration, calling the country's leaders weak, stupid, and ineffective. As one observer noted, "Trump's bravado, outrageousness and ego-driven persona was contrary to the tried and true Republican way of doing things."[2]

Throughout the campaign, various organizations would take polls, using samples of voters to rank the candidates in terms of their popularity. Most thought that with each controversial remark, Trump would sink in the polls and drop out of the race. They were wrong. To the surprise of most observers, as polling went forward, Trump's name began appearing at or near the top of poll after poll. In addition, Trump's unconventional views led to massive media coverage, giving him enormous free publicity on the television news networks and shows.

To many, Trump's brash speech and controversial comments seemed unpresidential. He was called "the most unconventional candidate in modern history."[3] But Trump supporters did not waver. To them he was a Washington outsider who had the life and business experience to turn Washington around.

> To many, Trump's brash speech and controversial comments seemed unpresidential.

The Primary Process

The primary voting process varies from state to state. In most states individuals vote directly for their choice of candidate. Other states hold caucuses where citizens meet in small groups to determine their choice of candidate. Still other states vote for delegates who will support their candidate of choice.

In September 2015, Trump participated in a debate with Republican candidates (*left to right*) Marco Rubio, Ted Cruz, Ben Carson, Jeb Bush, and Scott Walker.

•••••••••••••••••••

The Road to the Nomination

The first Republican primary was held in Iowa on February 1, 2016. Trump came in second, with Ted Cruz winning. Next came the New Hampshire primary, which Trump won handily. New Hampshire was followed by Nevada, South Carolina, and Alabama; all wins for Donald Trump. And his wins just continued. To the surprise of most, it began to appear that Trump might just win the Republican nomination.

And as his candidacy built momentum, his opponents began to drop out of the race. Trump turned his attention to those who remained, labeling them with unflattering

Looking Ahead

After becoming, against all conventional wisdom, the Republican nominee for president, Donald Trump faced his next hurdle to win the presidency. In the general election, to be held November 8, 2016, he would be running against a formidable Democratic nominee: former first lady, former US senator from New York, and former US secretary of state Hillary Rodham Clinton.

nicknames such as "Lyin' Ted" Cruz, "Low-Energy" Jeb Bush, and "Little Marco" Rubio. Once again, Trump was exhibiting a very unusual tactic for a presidential candidate. But against all odds, it seemed to be working. Trump continued to maintain his position at or near the top in each poll.

Traditional Republicans, along with the news media, were stunned by his success. And concerned. Because, even though he was running as a Republican, Trump paid little allegiance to the Republican Party and its leadership. From his viewpoint, he didn't need them to win.

On July 21, 2016, Donald J. Trump was named the Republican Party candidate for president. Against all odds, his win was considered by most to be "one of the most surprising victories in political hstory."[4] With that win, Trump's campaign efforts had only begun. His next goal would be to win the presidency.

Born to Win

. . . .

On June 14, 1946, Donald John Trump came into the world as the fourth child of Fred and Mary Trump. His siblings were Maryanne, Fred Jr. (called Freddy,) and Elizabeth. Two years later, Donald's younger brother, Robert, would join the family. The Trumps lived in Queens, New York, a mainly middle-class borough, or section, of New York City. As Donald grew up he became very proud of his parents; he was particularly close to his father.

Donald's Enterprising Father

Fred Trump's life had been a tough one, especially with his father's death from pneumonia when Fred was just thirteen years old. While his mother earned money as a seamstress, Fred, as the oldest son, was needed to help support his family financially. He was hardworking and enterprising and soon took on odd jobs, including working on construction sites, where he helped build houses. Finding that he

Donald Trump (*third from left*) grew up close to his parents. Here, he is posing with family members in 1985. From left to right are his younger brother, Robert; his father, Fred; his wife, Ivana; his sister Elizabeth; and his mother, Mary. Friend Roy Cohn joins them.

. . . .

enjoyed building, Fred also took evening classes in construction while he was still in high school.

By the time he was eighteen, Fred and his mother had formed a company called Elizabeth Trump & Son to develop and manage real estate. Fred needed his mother's help because at eighteen, he was too young to sign business contracts. He built his first home one year after graduating from high school, and he used the money he made when he sold it to build another home. Before long, Fred was in the business of building and selling homes in Queens. He specialized in building small brick homes that were reasonably priced. And his business only continued to expand. He either built new homes or bought and renovated homes that had been abandoned, turning them into rental properties. He made sure they were maintained well and enjoyed the monthly rental money that kept growing in his bank account. By the time Donald was born, Fred had become a very successful real estate developer. In addition to single-family homes, he also began to build or buy and renovate large middle-class apartment complexes in Queens and the Bronx, another nearby borough of New York City.

Fred built a large two-story home for his growing family on Midland Parkway in Queens. An imposing two-story brick home with a large porch supported by four tall white columns, the house had twenty-three rooms and nine bathrooms. Fred now had plenty of room for his growing children. As his business and wealth continued to grow over the years, the family also

The American Family Norm

The Trump family was typical for that time—a two-parent household in which his mother, Mary, stayed home and cared for the house and the children, while her husband, Fred, worked an outside job as a real estate developer. As Donald later wrote: "My father was the power and the breadwinner, and my mother was the perfect housewife."[1]

enjoyed the services of a maid, along with a chauffeur who drove their Cadillac limousine.

Donald Learns the Business from an Early Age

But success had its price for Fred. Donald remembers his father working constantly, from before dawn until after dark each day, seldom ever taking a day off. Not content to just sit back and pocket his monthly rental money, Fred knew that being successful meant keeping his properties well taken care of. And for him, that meant frequent personal inspections. As Donald grew older, he would often go with his father on weekends and school vacations to check on his properties. Together they would collect rents, inspect work in progress, and make sure everything was in excellent condition.

> He began to learn how to run a business well—it took constant attention and a lot of hard work.

Donald also had the job of scouting the ground for unused nails that could be recycled rather than wasted. All the while, Donald watched his father's behavior as a businessman, and it started to take hold. He began to learn how to run a business well—it took constant attention and a lot of hard work.

Donald also learned the value of a dollar by watching his father stretch his resources. For example, Fred might spray his apartment buildings for insects himself rather than paying someone to do it for him.

Donald also saw his father's reputation grow as a solid, dependable real estate developer.

Even though the Trump children grew up in relative wealth and in a large home, they did not feel particularly "rich."[2] Fred and Mary were determined not to spoil their children. They all had chores to do, and when they were old enough, all were required to get part-time jobs. Their parents ran a tight, structured

Located in the Jamaica Estates neighborhood of Queens, New York, his father built the imposing Trump family home when Donald was four years old. Trump lived in this home until he was twenty-five years old.

household with lots of rules. Money was not wasted on extra toys or frills.

Good behavior was also expected from the Trump children. Mary would report to Fred each evening about their children's behavior that day, and bad reports led to swift punishment. The Trump children were not allowed to own any pets. They had to go to their next door neighbors, the MacIntoshes, to get treats such as cookies or to cuddle their neighbor's cats and rabbits. The Trumps also taught their children to think positively, even when times were bad, and never to quit a job they had begun.[3]

As a boy growing up in the Trump household, Donald was full of energy and ambition. His older brother, Freddy, was not born with quite the same drive or killer instincts that Donald had. Instead, Freddy had a good sense of humor, enjoyed many friendships, and wanted to be liked. Their father saw Freddy as "soft" and did not respect him.[4]

> The Trumps also taught their children to think positively, even when times were bad, and never to quit a job they had begun.

He would constantly find fault with his oldest son's behavior and abilities, trying to make him tougher. Donald observed those harsh lessons and quickly learned what his father expected.[5] With his energy and ability to stand up to his father, Donald earned his father's respect. They would maintain a very close relationship for the rest of Fred's life.

Among his siblings, Donald was closest to his younger brother, Robert. Together they would play with blocks, each building his own skyscrapers and houses. Once, while playing with their blocks, Donald needed to borrow some of Robert's blocks to build an extra tall skyscraper. But rather than returning the borrowed blocks to his brother when he was through, Donald glued the pieces of his skyscraper together so he would never have to give them back. The incident served to predict Donald's ability to get what he wanted, a trait which would remain with him throughout his life.

Problem Child

Over time, Donald grew into a tall, blond boy. Along with his siblings, he attended Kew Forest, a private school about twenty minutes from the Trump home. He was not an excellent student, finishing in the bottom half of his elementary-school class. But he made up for low academics by excelling in athletics. Regardless of the sport, Donald proved to be a very competitive player, driven to win.

He was also somewhat of a discipline problem at Kew Forest. For example, he might set off a stink bomb in class, send spitballs flying across a classroom, or disrespectfully talk back to a teacher. Once, he was almost expelled for punching his music teacher in the face.

Donald Trump's senior picture from the New York Military Academy in Cornwall-on-Hudson, New York. His parents enrolled him in the academy when he was thirteen years old. They hoped a military environment would help channel Donald's energy in a positive way.

• •

As his older sister Maryanne remembered of that time, "He [Donald] was a brat."[6] Getting bad reports about their son's behavior at school did not please his parents. So when Donald was thirteen, they enrolled him in the New York Military Academy, a college preparatory boarding school about fifty-five miles (eighty-eight kilometers) north of New York City. Donald did not like the idea of attending military school.[7] But his father believed the academy would channel his son's energy in a more productive way. He hoped that in a military environment Donald would develop the self-discipline he needed.

Life was tightly structured at the academy. The students, or cadets as they were called, had to wear military uniforms every day. They awakened each morning before dawn to the piercing sound of a bugle, marched to their classes, and were expected to attend regular chapel services. While there, Donald was nicknamed "DT" by his classmates.

Donald easily could have rebelled against his newfound structure and limits. But luckily, he responded well. His father had been right. The new challenges at the academy tapped into Donald's competitive nature, and he drove himself to become the best cadet there. The athletic opportunities the academy offered appealed to Donald as well. While there he played football, soccer, basketball, and baseball. He earned a reputation as an outstanding first baseman and led the baseball team as its captain his senior year.

Meanwhile, Fred and Mary visited their son on weekends, watching as he matured. His high energy and training developed into self-confidence and leadership ability.

After graduating from New York Military Academy in 1964, Donald spent his next two years at Fordham University, a small men's school in the Bronx. At Fordham, he majored in business administration. While attending classes at Fordham, he lived at home and made reasonably good grades. He also put his athletic skills to use once again, playing squash, football, and tennis.

After two years at Fordham, Donald transferred to the University of Pennsylvania's Wharton School. Nationally known as one of the top business schools in the country, Wharton was yet another structured environment for Donald. Besides tough classes, Wharton had a formal atmosphere; its students had to wear coats and ties to classes. While there, Donald concentrated on real-estate classes. By the time he graduated from Wharton in 1968 with a bachelor's degree in economics, Donald Trump was ready to begin his career.

A Tough Competitor

· · · · · · · · · · · · · · · · · · ·

As his children grew, Fred Trump encouraged them to choose careers that they would love. Even so, he held out the hope that one of his sons might decide to join him in his business as a real estate developer.[1] And although Donald had briefly considered a career as a baseball player or as an actor earlier in his life, by the time he graduated from Wharton, he knew his destiny was in real estate.[2]

During this time, the United States was at war with North Vietnam in Southeast Asia. All men between the ages of eighteen and thirty-five faced the possibility of being drafted, or called upon by the government to serve in the armed forces to help with the war effort. Once he graduated from Wharton, Trump became eligible for the draft. But in September 1968, he was excused from any military obligation. Based on his physical examination by the draft office, he received a medical deferment. That meant that for medical reasons, he was excused from military duty.

His Father's Apprentice

For the next five years, Donald Trump worked directly with his father, learning more and more about the real-estate business. He lived at home for the first three years.

Donald Trump's father, Fred Trump, was a successful real estate developer in Queens and Brooklyn, New York. Fred taught Donald all about the real estate business and the value of hard work.

Together, every morning he and his father would go out to the Trump office on Avenue Z in the Bronx in Fred's chauffeur-driven limousine.

Always frugal and non-showy, Fred's office suited him just fine. Despite his wealth, he maintained a very low-key, nondescript place of business in a three-story brick building. Divided into cubicles, which served as offices for his employees, the Trump headquarters sported outdated 1950s furniture, a few plastic plants for decoration, linoleum floors, and shag carpeting.

Donald's addition to the company was just what his father had always hoped for. Fred's older son and namesake, Freddy, had tried to work for his father, but that had not gone well. Tough himself, Fred expected his sons to be, too—especially in business. Still ever critical of his oldest son, Fred continually criticized Freddy for not being tough enough to be a successful businessman.[3] Over time, the pressure and misery of working for his father became unbearable for Freddy. For comfort, he turned to smoking cigarettes and drinking alcohol excessively, which only made his father more furious.[4]

Once again, just as when he was a boy, Donald watched and learned from Freddy's mistakes. Observing his older brother's addictions to cigarettes and alcohol, he resolved never to drink alcohol or smoke himself, resolutions which he has kept throughout his life.

Eventually, Freddy left the real-estate business and moved to Florida, where he became an airline pilot. He left the job of working for Fred to his younger brother Donald, who was ready to go to work. As a friend of his father's noticed early on, Donald Trump's eagerness to get to work and make a name for himself was obvious. And in contrast to his father, who was always all business and serious, Donald Trump had a more open and friendly air about him.

Working at his father's side over the next five years, Donald Trump's duties mainly involved collecting rents and making sure the Trump properties were in top condition. Fred also used that time to complete his son's education in the art of successful real estate development.

There was a lot to learn, but Donald Trump was a quick study. Among his lessons, Fred taught his son how to collect rent from reluctant or even dangerous tenants. He learned the ins and outs of maintenance contracts and how to get the best deals on supplies. Fred also showed his son how to make all kinds of building repairs, so he would not have to hire a highly paid worker to do them. In addition, Fred also taught his son how to negotiate successfully with workers and unions and how to be tough to get his projects completed on time and within budget.

Over time, Donald Trump learned all the complexities of New York City real estate development, such as how to borrow money from banks to build a project, and how to deal successfully with the city zoning commissioners, whose job was to approve or deny new building proposals. He learned how to promote his projects and how to handle public opposition if that happened. And he learned the importance of using business contacts and political connections to his advantage.

As Donald Trump would later sum it up, "I learned about toughness [from my father] in a very tough business, I learned about motivating people, and I learned about competence and efficiency."[5]

Fred was also very careful about his appearance, another trait that his son would take on. Every day the two men wore suits or coats and ties, even on weekends. Fred made sure his son knew that a professional image was critical to a successful business.[6]

Out on His Own

In 1971, Donald Trump took the first step toward moving his career and dreams forward. He moved out of his family home on Midland Parkway and into a studio apartment on the Upper East Side of Manhattan. Living on the seventeenth floor of a twenty-one-story building, he called his tiny, dark new home with no view of the city his "penthouse."[7]

> "I learned about motivating people, and I learned about competence and efficiency."

Despite his modest dwelling, he was absolutely thrilled. "Moving into that apartment," he would later write, "was probably more exciting for me than moving, fifteen years later, into the top three floors of Trump Tower."[8] On his own for the first time, Donald Trump finally felt like he had entered the adult world, and he was proud to live in New York City. He also knew that he was where he needed to be to fulfill the next part of his dream—to get into big-time

Donald Trump moved from his family home to Manhattan when he was twenty-five years old. His first apartment in the city was modest. But to Trump, the move represented his first step toward fulfilling his dream of developing real estate in New York City.

• • • • • • • • • • • • • • • • • • • •

Manhattan real estate, selling to the world's wealthiest people.

Trump drove in style as well, owning a white Cadillac convertible. On the back bumper his customized license plate was printed with his initials—DJT. Each day, he would drive from Manhattan out to the Trump

Organization office on Avenue Z in the Bronx and return to Manhattan against rush-hour traffic each evening.

He also joined a posh private club in Manhattan called Le Club on East Fifty-eighth Street. Membership at Le Club meant success for him. He knew it would become a great place to meet and network with other businessmen,

Roy Cohn

Membership at Manhattan's exclusive Le Club put Donald Trump into contact with a man who would influence his life and business dealings nearly as strongly as his father had. Roy Cohn was a Manhattan attorney who had become notorious for being the right-hand man of Senator Joseph McCarthy during the infamous Red Scare in the 1950s.

After working for the government, Cohn went into private practice in New York, where he counseled a list of the city's heavy-hitters, both respected and not. After meeting Donald Trump at Le Club he became Trump's attorney, friend, and mentor. He introduced Trump to many of Manhattan's elite, helping him forge important business and social connections.

Cohn died in 1984, but his influence on Trump is evident even today, as seen in Trump's aggressive speeches, smearing of his opponents, and outlandish statements.

lawyers, bankers, and real estate developers—people who could help with his career.

Swifton Village

In 1972, Fred gave Donald the job of selling one of his apartment complexes in Cincinnati, Ohio. He had bought the complex in 1964, when his son was attending Fordham University. Built in the 1950s, the complex consisted of twelve hundred units, and it was one of the largest apartment complexes Cincinnati had to offer. It was called Swifton Village.

When Fred bought Swifton Village, most other real estate developers in the area thought it was a bad deal. The complex had not been well taken care of and had become rundown over the years. Many of the apartment units were vacant. But where others saw a disaster, Fred saw a great business opportunity.

He set to work hiring contractors to fix up the complex. Donald became familiar with the project and sometimes would fly over to Cincinnati with his father on weekends to help supervise and inspect the improvements as they progressed. Before long, with the help of fresh paint, new appliances, white shutters at the windows, and updated landscaping, new renters began flocking to the apartment complex.

But by the fall of 1972, Fred was ready to sell Swifton Village. The surrounding neighborhoods had declined, and many of his renters had decided to move elsewhere. By this time, he had enough confidence in his son's abilities to put him in charge of getting the complex sold. Before long, a possible buyer, Prudent

Real Estate Investment Trust, contacted Donald Trump to discuss the property. With the help of another apartment manager from the area, Trump convinced the Prudent representative that Swifton Village would be a great property to buy.

At twenty-six years of age, Donald Trump had successfully completed his first multimillion-dollar sale. It would be the first of many. Over time, he would occasionally offer his father business suggestions. Some his father took advantage of; others he did not. For example, Donald Trump convinced his father to refinance, or get new loans, for a number of his properties. That resulted in a savings of tens of thousands of dollars for the Trump Organization.

> **"I wanted to try something grander, more glamorous, and more exciting."**

But there was one piece of advice Donald was set on, while his father refused to budge: moving into Manhattan real estate. Fred was comfortable working the areas he was familiar with—Queens and the Bronx—where property values were reasonable, and most people had middle-class values and tastes.[9] But his son's sights were set on the glitz and glamour of Manhattan, home of some of the most expensive real estate in the world. "I learned very early on that I didn't want to be in the business my father was in [Queens and Brooklyn real estate]. I wanted to try something grander, more glamorous, and more exciting."[10]

Discrimination Charges

In 1973, the US Justice Department filed a lawsuit against the Trump Organization for discriminating against African Americans. The suit alleged that the Trump properties would not rent to African Americans, either falsely claiming that no apartments were available or quoting high rental rates, which they knew African American applicants could not afford. Fred had faced charges such as those years before, but had settled out of court with minimal publicity.

This time, however, his son took over and chose to confront the issue directly and publicly. True to the style for which he would become famous, Donald Trump called a press conference. He denied the charges and announced a countersuit against the government for $100 million in damages against the Trump Organization.

The case was finally settled two years later. By that time, Donald Trump's charges against the government had long been thrown out. The final ruling required the Trumps to advertise their apartments in a newspaper with a high African American readership; update the Urban League, a civil rights organization, on apartment vacancies; and count welfare payments when they were checking a possible tenant's income. By 1973, Fred was so pleased with his son's abilities as his assistant that he named him president of the company. Fred kept the title of chairman of the board.

Up to this time, Fred had called his company a variety of names, such as the Trump Village Construction Corporation or, in Cincinnati, the Swifton Land Corporation. Donald Trump convinced his father to formalize and finalize the name of the family company as the Trump Organization. It was simple and clear and remains the name of the company to this day.

Since his move to Manhattan, Donald Trump had kept constant watch on available real estate, waiting to find the right property for the right price. It had taken two years, but in 1973, the chance he had been waiting for opened up. Trump's career in high-end real estate was on the brink of taking off.

Making It Big

• •

Nineteen seventy-three was a year of financial decline for New York City. The city was not taking in enough income in taxes to be sure it could pay the city's employees. At the same time, property values in the city were in decline. It was a dismal time to be in the real estate business. But Trump was convinced that problems often could be turned into opportunities. And he was determined to use the bleak financial outlook to his advantage.[1]

And so he did. One day, while looking over the *New York Times* newspaper, Trump saw an article that caught his eye. The Penn Central Railroad had declared bankruptcy and was looking to sell its many properties, a number of which were in New York City.

Trump knew that with the company in financial distress, they would probably be willing to sell their holdings at a good price. So he called Penn Central's agent, Victor Palmieri, to find out more about the railroad's available property in New York City. One

Donald Trump points out details of his building plans for the Penn Central Railroad Yards in New York City. He is flanked by architects Jordan Gruzen (*left*) and Der Scutt (*right*).

• • • • • • • • • • • • • • • • • • • •

was an empty rail yard at Thirty-fourth Street; another was a rail yard at Sixtieth Street.

Over time, Trump convinced Palmieri to grant him the option to buy both rail yards. That meant that when it came time to develop, or build on, the properties, Trump would be the first to get the

34

chance to buy them. He was lucky to be working those deals. A complete unknown in the world of New York City real estate, he was a risky candidate to sell to. But he had several things going for him. First, his father's reputation as a dependable real-estate developer added to his credibility. Second, his energy and determination made a big positive impression on Palmieri. And finally, no other more qualified candidates came forward to make offers on the properties.

Trump had big plans for his new acquisitions. Between the two rail yards, he wanted to build a total of thirty thousand middle-income apartments in high-rise buildings. But he met with immediate opposition from the city planners who had to approve his proposal. Practically everyone thought Trump's idea was over-the-top and ridiculous.[2]

After fighting long and hard for city approval over the next several years, Trump finally released his option on the Thirty-fourth Street yards back to Penn Central. They then sold the property to the city, which used it to build a new convention center. It would be years before Trump's plans for the Sixtieth Street rail yard could go forward.

The Commodore Hotel

In the meantime, Trump's attention was caught by yet another Penn Central property, the Commodore Hotel on Forty-second Street. The Commodore had a long and glorious history. In its prime it had been regarded as one of New York City's finest landmarks.

The sixty-five-year-old hotel had been named for railroad businessman Cornelius (also known as Commodore) Vanderbilt. With 2,500 rooms, it was one of the largest hotels in New York City. But since its heyday, the Commodore had fallen on hard times.

Without enough money from Penn Central to keep it in good shape, the once grand hotel had become an eyesore. In fact, the whole area around Grand Central Terminal had fallen into decline. By the time the hotel got Trump's attention, it was rundown and dirty and surrounded by empty buildings and boarded-up storefronts. Few of its rooms were rented, and rumor had it that a section of the hotel was used to house a prostitution ring. Despite the Commodore's problems, Donald Trump saw it as a huge opportunity. He wanted to transform it back into the city's most glamorous hotel.[3]

But where Trump saw opportunity, practically everyone else saw disaster. His father, Fred, along with

A Grand Project

The Commodore was located across from Grand Central Terminal (often called Grand Central Station), one of the busiest railroad stations in the world. Because of that, the Commodore was in an excellent place to take advantage of the thousands of potential customers who flocked to the city each day on the trains that whizzed in and out of the station.

many others, told him they thought he was crazy to even consider buying the pitiful property.

Yet Trump was not discouraged. He knew there were many obstacles in his path, including getting city approvals. But he was not about to give up. As he would later write: "Winners see problems as just another way to prove themselves."[4] Instead, he focused on the possibility of success. If he was able to transform the Commodore and make it profitable, it would jump-start his reputation as a successful Manhattan real estate developer. He also knew that if the hotel did well, it would provide thousands of construction and service jobs for the city, and it would go a long way toward reversing the downturn of the entire Forty-second Street area.

> "Winners see problems as just another way to prove themselves."

Trump hired a lawyer, George Ross, to help him through the complexities he would need to overcome to make his plans for the hotel a reality. He also hired a well-known and respected architect named Der Scutt to develop a design for the hotel's new look.

Trump next needed to find a good hotel chain to partner with him in the Commodore project. Since he had no experience in hotel management, his job would be to renovate the hotel; theirs would be to manage it. Trump contacted the Hyatt Hotel organization to see if they might be interested. He knew that the chain was known for its quality, service, spectacular architecture, and profitable convention business. In addition, they did not already have a hotel in New York City.

In their talks with Trump, representatives from the Hyatt were not delighted with the New York City location he was proposing. Yet they knew he was also working on getting the Commodore a big tax break from the city, which would save them a lot of money.

So they agreed that if the project did, indeed, go forward, they would partner with Trump. The tax-break issue was critical. It would make or break the entire Commodore deal. To get it, Trump needed a big favor from the city of New York. He asked for a tax abatement for the hotel for the next forty years. That would mean that the hotel's owners would not have to pay property taxes on it during that time. If granted, it would save the hotel tens of millions of dollars. In exchange for the tax break, Trump offered the city a share of the hotel's profits.

The city officials were very reluctant to grant Trump a tax abatement. With the city nearly broke, they desperately needed the tax dollars a profitable hotel would provide. Also, once other hotel owners got wind of Trump's proposal, they protested that it would not be fair for the Commodore to get a tax break when other hotels did not. Along with the tax issue, Trump also needed to find a bank that would loan him the money to renovate the hotel. In all, he needed $70 million. But again, because of the city's strapped finances, banks were reluctant to loan money for any building project, much less to an unknown and untested real estate developer. Bank after bank turned him down. If they lent him the money and the Commodore project failed, they could lose all the money they had loaned him. So Trump continued to hammer away at the tax abatement issue. If he were successful with that, he thought a bank might be more willing to lend him money.[5]

The turning point with the city came in May 1976 when Penn Central announced its plan to completely close the Commodore in just six days. That prompted the city to act in Trump's favor. The last thing they wanted was the negative publicity of a well-known hotel shutting down in the city. In addition, Trump and his father had strong connections with the governor of New York at the time, Hugh Carey, along with the mayor of New York City, Abe Beame. With their backing, the tax abatement was approved. That breakthrough paved the way for the bank loans Donald Trump needed.

Building a Family

In the meantime, since his move to Manhattan in 1971, Trump had not taken the time to include romance in his life. He sometimes dated models he met at Le Club, but none had turned into a serious relationship. He was too focused on getting his career off the ground.[6] But his social life changed dramatically in the summer of 1976. Still not a serious dater, one night Trump stopped in at Maxwell's Plum, a popular restaurant on the Upper East Side, for dinner. As fate would have it, that night he happened to cross paths with a strikingly beautiful, twenty-seven-year-old blond model from Canada, named Ivana Marie Zelnickova Winklmayr.

Donald and Ivana Trump are photographed in their Manhattan apartment in 1979. They would work together on building projects and have three children—Donald Jr., Ivanka, and Eric.

She, along with several other models, was trying to get a table at the crowded restaurant. Trump came to their rescue, not only getting them a table, but also picking up their bill. After later escorting the ladies back to their hotel, Trump sent Ivana roses the next day. Indeed, she had Trump's interest.

Ivana had immigrated to Canada from Czechoslovakia (now the Czech Republic) three years earlier, where she became a successful fashion model. When she met Trump, she was in New York City for a modeling assignment. Shortly after they met, the couple began to date whenever she was in the city.

And Trump did everything he could to sweep her off her feet.

As he got to know her better, Trump found that he and Ivana shared many of the same qualities. Like him, she was self-confident, competitive, and driven to excel.[7] She also had a tremendous amount of energy and was quite intelligent.[8] That fall, he took her to Queens to meet his parents.

An expert skier, Ivana was involved with another man, George Syrovatka, when she met Trump. Like her, Syrovatka was also an excellent skier, and he sold sports equipment in Montreal, Canada. He had been responsible for helping Ivana emigrate from Czechoslovakia. But Trump, used to getting what he wanted, turned Ivana's head. At twenty-seven, she was ready to get married, and she knew George was not. So when Trump proposed on New Year's Eve 1976, Ivana said yes.

The couple was married on April 9, 1977, at the Marble Collegiate Church in New York City. Following the small ceremony, which included the couple's immediate families and a few close friends, Trump and his bride enjoyed an elegant reception at the exclusive 21 Club. The Trumps then honeymooned in exotic Acapulco, Mexico.

Once home from his honeymoon, Trump jumped back into the fray to keep the Commodore project moving forward. That same year, the Trumps welcomed their first child, Donald John Trump Jr., into the world on December 31. They called him Donny.

The Trumps Take Manhattan

Trump's first real estate development in Manhattan was the Grand Hyatt Hotel. Its flashy glass exterior and renovated interior became a glamorous place for visitors to stay.

Construction on the Commodore began in June 1978. With the help of his architect, Der Scutt, Trump was now ready to make his vision for the hotel come to life. For the exterior of the building he used reflective glass. It immediately updated the hotel's look and made it gleam with flash and glamour. Next, he gutted the building's interior and rebuilt it with 1,400 larger rooms, rather than its previous 2,500 tiny rooms. And finally, he created a spectacular lobby. It was several stories high, and decorated with lush plants and fountains. He also installed a warm brown-colored marble for the floor, along with shiny brass railings and columns. In addition, he built a glass-enclosed restaurant, which projected over Forty-second Street. The renovated hotel was called the Grand Hyatt. It would be one of the few Trump properties that did not bear the Trump name.

The hotel's renovation took over a year. As the project moved forward, Donald Trump established his work habits. Just like his father, Fred, he worked constantly. He used travel time in his chauffeur-driven silver Cadillac limousine to catch up on telephone calls. An assistant often rushed papers needing his signature to wherever he might be having lunch. And Trump's lunches were either business related or nonexistent. When he was free for lunch, he might not eat at all or else he would grab a quick sandwich to eat while he worked.

Trump's lifelong high energy and drive kept him going. Even sleep did not slow him down—he could function just fine with very little. Trump's style with his employees was typically positive and upbeat. Convinced that he only hired the best, he treated his staff well. That is, unless mistakes were made. When that happened, Trump's temper could be ferocious. Yet, his employees knew how hard their boss worked and that he expected their best efforts. They either gave that or found another company to work for.

Meanwhile, Ivana Trump got involved with New York City's elite social set by volunteering to raise money for charities. She was also responsible for establishing her husband's nickname, "the Donald." Her native Czech language does not require articles, such as "a" and "the" as we do in English. So when speaking English, she often put articles in front of nouns whether they were needed or not. Speaking in her heavily accented English in an interview with the *New York Times*, Ivana said, "The Donald is fantastic in the golf and very good in the tennis."[9] The phrase stuck, and from then on he has often been referred to as "the Donald."

Ivana was also interested in her husband's real estate business. Once renovation began at the Commodore, she enjoyed visiting the work site, wearing expensive designer dresses and high heels, along with a hard hat. Before long, Trump put his wife in charge of the building's interior design.

Not surprisingly, her presence was rather distracting for the construction workers. She was also criticized for interfering with business decisions and being overbearing.[10] But "the Donald" loved that his very capable wife was interested in his work. Not only did he approve of her decorating work, he also saw her on-site presence as giving him an extra set of eyes and ears so he would always know what was going on.

Once the Commodore renovation was completed, the thirty-four-story Grand Hyatt opened in November 1980 with great fanfare. And true to Trump's vision, it was a big success from the first.[11] At the same time, his dream of becoming a recognized and respected "player" in Manhattan real estate was coming true.

To the Top of the Tower

· · · · · · · · · · · · · · · ·

Fifth Avenue at Fifty-sixth Street in Manhattan was another location that had drawn Trump's attention. It would become the location of his favorite, and most famous property, Trump Tower.[1]

Trump had long had his eye on the site. But it was occupied by the Bonwit Teller building. It was an eleven-story limestone structure, which housed the Manhattan branch of the well-known and high-end department store. The building had been built in 1929. As with the Commodore, Trump was not discouraged by the complexities of getting his new project built on that site. As he later wrote: "I aim very high, and then I just keep pushing . . . to get what I'm after."[2]

First Steps

Indeed, he would push for years to get his tower built. First, he called Bonwit Teller's owner, Franklin Jarman, offering to buy the building. But he was turned down. After that, he would send a letter or call again every six months or so just to see if Jarman had changed his mind. He had not, until one day in 1978: Trump read that Genesco, Incorporated, the parent company for Bonwit Teller, was having financial difficulties and was interested in selling some of its properties.

This time, Trump's offer to buy the building was accepted. Along with the building itself, the $25 million deal also included the lease for the land it was on. About the deal, Trump would later write, "sheer persistence [can be] the difference between success and failure."[3]

Trump knew that buying the Bonwit Teller land lease was not good enough. It meant that the land was just rented; he did not own it. And the lease was due to expire in just twenty-nine years. The last thing Trump needed was to construct a big building on the property, only to risk having it torn down by the landowner when the land lease expired. So his next move was to contact the owner of the land, the Equitable Life Assurance Society, to see if they would sell it. They agreed to sell the land. In exchange, Trump gave them half ownership in what would become his new building. Next, Trump wanted to buy rights to the air space above the building next door, the famous Tiffany and Company jewelry store. He needed that to create the giant-sized building he envisioned. So he met with Tiffany's owner, Walter Hoving, and convinced him to sell Tiffany's air rights for $5 million. By the end of 1978, Trump had all the land issues resolved for his new building. A *New York Times* article would note, "That Mr. Trump was able to obtain the location . . . is testimony to [his] persistence and to his skills as a negotiator."[4]

The Most Fantastic Building in New York

At that point, despite all the progress he had made, Trump's work had only begun. Ahead of him lay all the intricate maneuvering through the complexities of New York City's real estate transactions. Trump knew that for the kind of high-profile skyscraper he wanted to build, he would need lots of variances, or special permissions, from the city.

Once again, Trump hired his Grand Hyatt architect, Der Scutt, to develop a design for the tower. Always aiming high, he told Scutt, "I want to build the most fantastic building in New York."[5] Scutt sketched dozens of designs for the building's exterior. Trump reviewed them and chose the parts he liked from each. He later wrote: "Without a unique design, we'd never get approval for a very big building."[6]

> "I aim very high, and then I just keep pushing . . . to get what I'm after."

He wanted his new project to be as tall as possible. That would provide more space for condominiums, which would give the Trump Organization maximum profits. In addition, Trump knew that the views of Central Park and the New York City skyline would be critical for getting the condominiums sold at the highest possible prices.

From the first, Trump and Scutt decided not to go with a straight boxlike skyscraper. The final design for the building was something different—a saw-toothed, or zigzagged, design. It was not only unusual, but gave

Donald Trump displayed photographs of the Bonwit Teller building (*foreground*) along with his vision for its replacement, Trump Tower (*background.*) His dream for Trump Tower would take five years to become a reality.

the building twenty-eight sides. Trump was delighted, because each side provided another view of the city.

But first, New York's City Planning Commission had to approve the design. And that would not be easy. One problem was that the building Trump proposed—a flashy high-rise—was a drastic departure from the other buildings in that area. Most were built of limestone or brick and were around fifty years old. In contrast, Trump wanted his building's exterior to be a smoky gray glass.

In addition, Trump was proposing a new concept— a multiuse building. The first six stories would be an enclosed shopping mall with exclusive retail stores. The next six floors would be office buildings. And the remaining stories would be constructed as high-end, very expensive, luxury condominiums.

As expected, the city planners objected to the building's design, and the project was at a standstill until two things happened. First, Trump had Scutt prepare a model for the tower that would meet all the Planning Commission's requirements. When they saw it, even they were disappointed and realized it would not be an asset to the city's architecture. Second, the highly respected *New York Times* newspaper's architecture critic, Ada Louise Huxtable, reviewed the Trump-preferred design. In an article entitled "A New York Blockbuster of Superior Design," Huxtable praised the plan for the building, writing: "A great deal of care has . . . been lavished on its design. It is undeniably a dramatically handsome structure."[7]

After that, Trump's plan was unanimously approved by the city in 1979. With 263 condominiums, it would be New York City's tallest residential building. Chase Manhattan Bank agreed to loan Trump $200 million to build his tower.

Trump knew it would be very expensive to build, but he was convinced that the luxury it afforded would quickly attract clients willing and able to pay top dollar for a spectacular place to live. He hired a woman named Barbara Res to manage the tower's construction. He had seen her work on the Grand Hyatt construction crew

Bonwit Teller

The Bonwit Teller department store was founded in New York City in 1895 by German businessman Paul Bonwit. Two years later, Bonwit took Edmund Teller as his partner and Bonwit Teller became known as a purveyor of high-end women's apparel.

Through the years, as the city's upscale shopping districts moved uptown, Bonwit Teller followed suit, landing at its final location on Fifth Avenue at Fifty-sixth Street in 1930. Its success allowed the company to open branch locations in other cities, catering to the wealthy and well-dressed.

Bonwit Teller began its decline in the 1970s. When Donald Trump purchased its Fifth Avenue building, the store moved to another location but was unable to recapture its glory days. The company, which had transferred ownership over the years, filed for bankruptcy in 1989. Its last remaining branch closed in 2000.

and was impressed with her ability. He admired her take-charge attitude and lack of intimidation when working with the tough, mostly male construction workers. When Trump hired her, she became the first woman to be put in charge of constructing a skyscraper in New York City.

The Dream Becomes Reality

Demolition of the Bonwit Teller building began on March 15, 1980. The building had been graced with two bas-relief sculptures above the eighth floor. Bas-relief means that the sculptures were attached to the building, but they were raised slightly from its surface. They were considered by some to be valuable, as well as important from an architectural standpoint. A representative from New York City's Metropolitan Museum of Art had contacted Trump about the possibility of saving the sculptures, along with the iron grille work above the entrance to the store. They hoped that Trump would consider donating the artwork to the museum. Trump agreed. However, by the time the building was being torn down, his demolition crew advised him that the sculptures were very heavy and would be difficult to remove. It would take a lot of extra time and money to get them down without damaging them. The result was that the sculptures were destroyed. Neither was the grille work saved. That created a lot of negative publicity for Trump. But over time, the storm passed.

Trump was rather surprised by all the negative press he received about the sculptures. He later wrote: "Despite what some people may think, I'm not looking to be a bad guy when it isn't absolutely necessary."[8] Still, looking at the bright side, he saw the publicity as free advertising for his new building.

Trump wanted the tower's atrium, or open lobby, to be spectacular. And he got his wish. By this time, he had hired Ivana as executive vice president in charge of interior design for the Trump Organization. As with the Grand Hyatt, she was responsible for the interior decorating decisions for the building. She chose a rare and beautiful peach-colored marble for the atrium's walls and floor. It was very expensive and would require expert marble cutters to handle it. Ivana went to Italy herself to supervise the job of quarrying the marble. That way she could make sure the tones would match. In all, the Trumps imported 240 tons of the special marble for the Trump Tower atrium. Along with the striking marble, Ivana used highly polished bronze for the atrium's columns and escalators. Lots of live greenery, including flowers, trees, and shrubs, was also added. At the same time, the atrium contained a spectacular eighty-foot-high (twenty-four-meter-high) waterfall, which added to the dramatic effect of the area. Trump saw the elegance and flair of the atrium as a "symbol of the Trump Organization."[9]

> [I]f you are a little different, or a little outrageous . . . the press is going to write about you."

As construction moved forward, Ivana's famous attention to the tiniest details of the interior paid off. The atrium would later receive an architectural award

for excellence from the Fifth Avenue Association. The building's entrance on Fifth Avenue was dramatically oversized, measuring 30 feet (9 m) wide. Above the doors, "Trump Tower" was prominently displayed in two-foot-high (sixty centimeter) letters in brass.

By this time, Trump had become well known enough in New York City to be interesting to the media. He used his name well to advertise his projects. Later he explained, "If you are a little different, or a little outrageous . . . the press is going to write about you."[10] Trump realized that his attention in the media was as good as paid advertising to get the word out about his buildings. He also believed in the art of exaggeration, writing that it is "a very effective form of promotion."[11]

The five-story Trump Tower atrium is a dramatic display combining pink marble, glass, and polished bronze. Its opulence is intended to attract shoppers, visitors, and tourists.

For example, Trump Tower is advertised as being sixty-eight stories tall, while in reality, it only has fifty-eight floors.

Despite all he had accomplished with the Grand Hyatt and Trump Tower projects, Donald Trump was not always warmly accepted by many of the other real-estate developers in the area. They tended to be more conservative and reserved, a style that generally suited their clients. Trump, on the other hand, was young and thought of as brash and too flashy in his appearance and personality.[12] Still, he received grudging respect for his important real estate successes.[13]

Selling Fantasy

In the middle of all the Trumps' work on the tower, their lives changed again on October 30, 1981, with the birth of their second child, Ivanka Marie. On top of that, Trump also bought and renovated yet another building, to be called Trump Plaza. Located on Third Avenue, it provided another option for wealthy clients—this time in an apartment cooperative in which the tenants shared part ownership in the building itself.

Ivana once again helped her husband with the Trump Plaza's interior design, as well as with monitoring the construction to make sure the building was completed on time. It would eventually become home to such celebrities as Dick Clark and Martina Navratilova.

The next year the Trumps began scouting the area for a weekend getaway home. They found what they were looking for in nearby Greenwich, Connecticut. The forty-three-year-old redbrick home with white shutters was situated on five acres (two hectares) of land. It also had a glassed-in back porch that overlooked the harbor below. Once they bought it, Ivana set to work getting the home renovated and updated for her family.

Trump Tower officially opened in February 1983, with lots of media fanfare. Trump marketed his condominiums to celebrities as well as to wealthy people from foreign countries. Ultimately, his tenants would include talk-show host Johnny Carson, movie director Steven Spielberg, entertainer and pianist Liberace, and singer Paul Anka.

Trump's most powerful selling feature for his condominiums at Trump Tower was the spectacular and unique views they provided of Central Park, the Manhattan skyline, the Statue of Liberty, and the East

Two-foot-tall (sixty-centimeters-tall) brass letters announce Trump Tower to visitors. The building would become Trump's favorite and most famous creation. It also quickly became a landmark and tourist attraction for New York City.

and Hudson Rivers. For maximum views Trump built the apartments with huge windows that ran almost from ceiling to floor. He also charged the highest prices ever for condominiums in the city. Beginning at $5 million for a one-bedroom, the price tag rose to $11 million for a three-story triplex. "We positioned ourselves as . . . the hottest ticket in town. We were selling fantasy," he would later write.[14]

For the building's atrium, Trump rented space to some of the most prestigious retail stores in the world, including Cartier, Martha, and Harry Winston. Shoppers at Trump Tower could buy anything from expensive jewelry to fine crystal and valuable antiques.

The building was an immediate success. Its condominiums sold quickly and the spectacular building drew lots of tourists. With the building's taxes, its stores, the condominiums, and the thousands of jobs it provided, Trump Tower became a huge financial bonus for New York City. Once the tower was completed, Trump and his family moved in as well, taking one of the two triplexes at the top of the building. Ivana had worked hard to make their new home especially luxurious. Using a lot of marble, gold leaf, and crystal chandeliers, Trump wanted the quality and opulence of his Trump Tower home to equal that of Versailles Palace outside of Paris, France.[15]

Later, he would combine his triplex with the other penthouse triplex in the tower, creating a gigantic home with fifty rooms. The 80-foot-long (24 m) living room provides panoramic views of Central Park, and it includes twenty-seven hand-carved marble columns, along with a 12-foot-high (3 m) fountain.

Trump also converted space on the twenty-sixth floor of the tower into offices for the Trump Organization, where they remain today. Three walls of his office are floor-to-ceiling glass, providing panoramic views of the city. Ivana took over an office next to her husband's. With Trump Tower, Donald Trump's longtime dream of owning high-end Manhattan real estate had come true. He made it happen using a combination of vision, determination, and perseverance, along with a bit of luck. He still had many new projects ahead of him, both in and outside the world of Manhattan real estate.

Spreading
the Wealth

· · · · · · · · · · · · · · · ·

T rump's reputation as an important real estate developer began to grow. Between the Grand Hyatt and Trump Tower, Trump had proved that he could successfully complete major building projects and maneuver the complexities the deals required. He was known to take big risks, which, if they worked out, only added to his success. But failure could easily mean public humiliation and huge financial losses.

At the same time, Trump was courting, and getting, a lot of media attention, not only in New York City, but across the country. In 1983, articles about him began to appear in national magazines such as *Town and Country*, *GQ*, and *People*. With two young children, a beautiful wife helping him, and two spectacular homes, Donald Trump seemed to have it all. So, what was next for "the Donald"? As it turned out, more than even he might have imagined. Shortly after Trump Tower opened, Trump decided to get involved in the world of professional football.

The New Jersey Generals

The United States Football League (USFL), organized the previous year, was a struggling league whose teams played their games in the spring. That way, they would not have to compete for fans against the powerful National Football League's (NFL) annual fall/winter season. In 1983, Trump bought one of the USFL's teams, the New Jersey Generals.

But the USFL was having a hard time. Without many nationally recognized players, most of the USFL teams had small fan bases. And that meant the teams were not bringing in much money.

By the end of their second season, the league was in serious financial trouble. But with Trump on board as a USFL team owner, he wanted to change all that. First, he thought the league should play in the fall and compete directly against the NFL. Second, he was convinced that if the USFL teams signed nationally known players away from the NFL, that the league's fan base would expand. Ultimately, he hoped that the USFL teams would merge with the NFL. If that happened, the value of his team, the Generals, would skyrocket. But if the USFL was not successful, Trump thought they should file a lawsuit against the NFL, charging that the NFL was a monopoly. A monopoly is a situation in which one company, in this case the NFL, controls an industry, preventing any competition. If the USFL won that case, Trump thought they would get a big cash settlement, which could help them hire more high-profile players and continue on.

Taking a Gamble on a Casino

Meanwhile, Trump's attention also took him back to real estate—this time in Atlantic City, New Jersey. Just 125 miles (201 km) from New York City, Atlantic City had become second only to Las Vegas as a center for high-stakes gambling.

Trump knew gambling could be a very profitable business, and he had thought for years that he might

want to get involved in it. So he went to Atlantic City to investigate. At the same time he was working on the Grand Hyatt back in New York City, he found property he was interested in on the Atlantic City Boardwalk. Actually, the land Trump wanted was made up of three separate pieces of property, with a total of thirty different owners. But Trump was not put off by the problems it would take to buy the land. He was ready to move forward to put the deals together.

Before long, Trump had acquired his boardwalk property and had hired his younger brother, Robert, to manage it. But the casino he planned to build there would be delayed for several

Trump turned his attention to the gambling industry in Atlantic City, New Jersey, where he began to invest in renovating and developing casinos and hotels.

years because he could not find a bank to loan him the money to build it. Banks were skeptical about loaning money for casinos, viewing them as a high-risk business.

It would take a couple of years, but finally Trump's luck changed. He was contacted by the Holiday Inn hotel chain. They already had a very successful casino, Harrah's, open in Atlantic City, but it was not on the boardwalk. And Holiday Inn wanted to own a casino/hotel on the boardwalk, where most of the tourists and gamblers spent their time. So they suggested a partnership with Trump. Holiday Inn would finance the building on Trump's property, and Trump would build it.

The new casino/hotel opened in 1984. It was called Harrah's at Trump Plaza. The opening was a gala event, with an estimated nine thousand people attending. In the meantime, the USFL lawsuit against the NFL was filed in late 1984. The USFL sought $1.32 billion in damages. After two years in court, the USFL won their suit. But to their dismay, the jury only awarded them one dollar in damages. With dwindling funds and a decreasing fan base, the USFL folded. Nevertheless, Trump's national media exposure only increased because of his participation with the USFL. For example, in 1984 his picture was on the cover of the *New York Times Magazine*, with an accompanying article entitled: "The Expanding Empire of Donald Trump." Within the lengthy article, the author wrote: "Donald J. Trump is the man of the hour."[1] And Trump loved the media attention. He knew it promoted not only his properties, but his personal fame as well. Nineteen eighty-four was also a special year for the Trumps with the addition of their third child, Eric.

As a father, Trump is quick to admit that when his children were young he was not very comfortable spending time with them and playing with them.[2] He left most of the parenting to their mother, Ivana, whom he often praised as a wonderful mother. But as his children grew older, he became more involved with them. And despite his hectic schedule, he enjoyed their frequent telephone calls.

Trump Castle and Trump Parc

The next year, Trump was once again back in Atlantic City. His activity there was far from over. His next acquisition would be property he bought from the Hilton Hotel Corporation. When he bought it in 1985, the property was already well under construction. Trump was able to buy it because the Hilton Corporation had unexpectedly been denied a gambling license by Atlantic City's Casino Control Commission. Without that, the Hilton Corporation could not own or operate a casino there, so they needed to sell their building.

> Within the lengthy article, the author wrote: 'Donald J. Trump is the man of the hour.'

The hotel/casino contained 615 hotel rooms, along with a large casino floor. Trump bought the property for $320 million. Then he finished the construction and named his new property Trump Castle. It opened in June 1985. Trump put his wife, Ivana, in charge of managing it.

For her new job, Ivana would commute several days each week from New York City to Atlantic City in the Trump helicopter. She arrived early each morning, took care of hotel business, and would return to New York City in the evenings to spend time with her children.

Along with his interest in Atlantic City, Trump continued to scout Manhattan for property to buy and develop. Several years earlier, he had added two more buildings to his growing empire. One was an old apartment building at 100 Central Park South. The other was the Barbizon Hotel next door. Trump's plan was to tear both buildings down and replace them with a luxurious hotel and shops. But he ran into problems with the people living in the apartment building. The main problem was that the building was rent-controlled. That meant that the rent its tenants paid was protected and kept very low by state and city laws. The laws had been put in place years earlier to provide affordable housing in the city.

In addition, the apartments at 100 Central Park South were lovely, with high ceilings, large rooms, and magnificent views of Central Park and the city. And because of rent control, the tenants were getting their exquisite homes at bargain prices.

So when the tenants of 100 Central Park South learned of Trump's plans to tear their building down, they were furious. They organized together, hired a lawyer, and filed a lawsuit against him, claiming that he could not tear down their building and force them to find new homes.

Trump, true to his style, fought back for several years. But in 1985, he finally gave in; the building would remain. In addition, he would renovate it, as well as the Barbizon Hotel next door, converting it into luxury condominiums, and renaming it Trump Parc.

Even though his plans for 100 Central Park South did not go as he had planned, Trump turned the outcome into a victory for himself, publicly saying the tenants had helped him. He said he had saved lots of money by simply renovating the buildings, rather than building a new one.

Mar-a-Lago

Also in 1985, the Trumps bought the spectacular Mar-a-Lago estate in Palm Beach, Florida. Mar-a-Lago, which means "Sea-to-Lake" in Spanish, had been built by Marjorie Merriweather Post, heiress to the Post breakfast food fortune. The mansion had taken four years to build, and was completed in 1927.

A magnificent estate, it had 118 rooms, including 58 bedrooms, 33 bathrooms, 27 servants' rooms, a movie theater, and a dining room that could seat as many as 50 guests. Trump bought the Spanish-Mediterranean-style property for $5 million. He paid an extra $3 million for the home's furnishings, along with its tableware, which would accommodate up to two hundred guests. The Mar-a-Lago grounds already had a tennis court, and the Trumps would add a swimming pool and a nine-hole golf course.

Trump bought the Mar-a-Lago (meaning "Sea-to-Lake") property in 1985. Located in exclusive Palm Beach, Florida, the sprawling, seventeen-acre (six-hectare) estate has fifty-eight bedrooms. The mansion was built by Marjorie Merriweather Post, former owner of General Foods, Inc.

• •

The home became a winter retreat for the family, as well as a special place to entertain friends and business associates. Trump also turned the estate into a private club. With membership fees at $150,000, club members could schedule Mar-a-Lago for their personal use.

At the same time, Trump formed a partnership with Lee Iacocca, chairman of the Chrysler Corporation. Together they bought a condominium complex in Palm Beach, which they named Trump Plaza of the Palm Beaches.

Helping the City

Back in New York City, in the spring of 1986, Trump turned his attention to the Wollman Skating Rink in Central Park. Built in 1950, the rink was owned by the city, and it was one of the largest outdoor skating rinks in the world. But it had been closed for repairs in 1980. By 1986, after $13 million and six years, those repairs still were not finished, and the once-popular rink remained closed.

Trump was disgusted with what he considered the city's embarrassing failure to get the rink back up and running again.[3] In May 1986, he offered to take over the renovation at cost, meaning he would make no profit on the project. He knew it would give him a lot of positive publicity in the city, something he craved and enjoyed.

Under Trump's supervision, the rink reopened in November 1986, having come in under budget and ahead of schedule. A sure media hit, Trump arranged for many of the world's most prominent skaters, including Peggy Fleming and Dorothy Hamill, to be at the opening ceremonies.

As with the renovation of the Grand Hyatt, Trump came off not only as a great real estate developer, but also as a hero for New York City. A news article praised him for helping "lead the city out of the darkness of the mid-1970s."[4]

More Changes and Expansion

During this time, Ivana and her husband's relationship was taking a downturn. Their competitive natures had become a problem—they had begun to compete against each other.[5] In addition, they enjoyed different things. She loved champagne, fancy meals, and high-society parties. He, on the other hand, had more simple tastes in food, hated the small talk required at parties, and liked to go to bed early.

By 1987, Trump's head was turned by another beautiful blonde, Marla Maples. When they met, she was twenty-three; he was forty. From Dalton, Georgia, she was a beauty pageant winner, a swimsuit model, and an aspiring actress. Unknown to Ivana, Trump and Marla became romantically involved.

Also in 1987, Trump added the world of publishing to his activities by writing, with the help of Tony Schwartz, his first book. He had been approached by Random House publishers to write his autobiography. The resulting book was called *Trump: The Art of the Deal*. It quickly became a best seller.

To celebrate, Trump held what he would call, "The Party of the Year" at Trump Tower. Among the two thousand guests who attended were such celebrities as Barbara Walters and Michael Douglas, along with prominent New York politicians and Trump business associates. In addition, he made the interview circuit, promoting his book on a number of television talk shows.

Ever on the alert to add to his holdings, in 1987 Trump bought the world's third largest yacht, which he named the *Trump Princess*. It cost him $29 million. The yacht contained eleven ultra-luxury guest suites, each named for a different precious or semiprecious stone. The magnificent yacht also had two waterfalls, a helipad, three elevators, and a three-bed infirmary, along with living quarters for more than fifty servants.

Countrywide Attention

More and more people across the country began to recognize Donald Trump's name. National magazines printed articles about him. He also appeared as a guest on talk shows such as *Larry King Live* and *Late Night with David Letterman*.

Despite his purchase, Trump was not fond of boating and never spent a night on the luxury yacht. He would later admit, "It makes me nervous to relax."[6] Instead, he used the yacht to entertain clients and high-roller gamblers from his casinos in Atlantic City. At the same time, he started making plans to sell the *Trump Princess* and build an even bigger and more opulent yacht.[7]

The next year, Trump bought the world-famous Plaza Hotel in New York City. Built in 1907, the luxury hotel was located along Central Park South in Manhattan. It had been built to look like a French chateau, or small castle. Considered a New York City landmark, the hotel was also well known as the setting for the famous Eloise children's book series by Kay Thompson. In addition, the building was used as part of the set in a number of movies, including *Home Alone 2: Lost in New York*.

Trump paid approximately $400 million for the Plaza. It was a price he knew was too high. But in an article published in the *New York Times*, he explained, "This isn't just a building. It's the ultimate work of art. I was in love with it."[8]

After buying the Plaza, Trump transferred Ivana from Trump Castle in Atlantic City back to New York City to manage his latest purchase and oversee its renovation. The next spring, Trump also expanded into the airline industry. He bought twenty-one Boeing 727 airplanes from Eastern Airlines Shuttle, renaming them Trump Air. After updating and improving the interior of the planes, they became his shuttle service, which carried airline commuters between New York City, Boston, and Washington, DC.

That same year, Trump suffered a tremendous business loss when his three top casino executives were killed in a helicopter crash in October. They were on their way to Atlantic City after a meeting with Trump earlier that morning in New York City. He was devastated personally and professionally by the tragedy, later writing: "I felt sadder than I've ever felt in my life."[9]

> **"This isn't just a building. It's the ultimate work of art. I was in love with it."**

Despite the tragic loss to the Trump Organization, business continued. Back in Atlantic City, Trump's most spectacular property there would become the Trump Taj Mahal hotel and casino. He bought it for a reported $273 million when it was half finished and would spend more than $500 million to complete it. It became one of the world's largest casinos, with 3,000 slot machines and 160

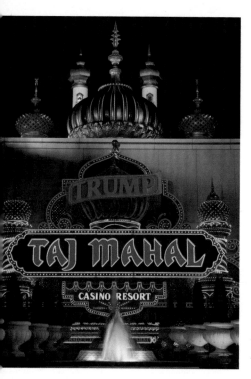

Trump bought the unfinished Taj Mahal Hotel and Casino in 1987. At its 1990 opening, Trump proclaimed the Taj Mahal the "Eighth Wonder of the World."

gaming tables. On the downside, the spectacular property needed to take in $1.3 million from its customers each day just to keep the building operating and its employees paid.

The Trump Taj Mahal opened in April 1990, billed as the "Eighth Wonder of the World." The opening night ceremonies were dramatic and spectacular. With hundreds of people attending and lots of publicity, Trump began by rubbing an Aladdin's lamp, after which a genie appeared, followed by a laser show and fireworks.

By 1990, Donald Trump's empire was enormous and diverse. But trouble loomed ahead. It would become almost more than even he could handle.

Running on Empty

. . . .

T he value of real estate in the country tends to run
in cycles. Some years the value of property is high,
and so its prices are, too. On the other hand, real estate
can also sink into a depression, when property values
and prices drop.

In the late 1980s and early 1990s, real estate values
dropped across the country. With that, income for
Trump's buildings dropped as well. He could no longer
charge as much for his luxury condominiums. On top of
that, his casino businesses were not bringing in as much
money as he needed to cover the payments on the huge
bank loans he had taken out to build them.

Trump blamed his casino problems on Atlantic
City. First, the city's cold winter weather sent potential
gamblers to warmer climates for a large part of each year.
And second, he saw the city itself as not very appealing
to visitors. Instead, he thought it looked rundown and
depressed.[1]

In addition, with the loss of his three top casino executives, Trump's chances of handling his money crisis only worsened. Suddenly, with dwindling income, Trump could not make his monthly loan payments to the banks. And once that happened, he was in danger of losing his buildings and having the banks take them over. Because of his name and reputation, banks had loaned Trump more than they should have.[2] He was very close to bankruptcy.

Trump was certainly not the only real-estate developer facing financial ruin during that time. Many others were as well, and a number of them were forced to declare bankruptcy.

More Bad News

At the same time that Trump's financial world was falling apart, his marriage was, as well. Ivana found out about his ongoing relationship with Marla Maples and filed for divorce. The Trumps had signed a prenuptial, or before marriage, agreement stating which Trump assets Ivana would get if she and her husband ever did, indeed, divorce. But by this time, Ivana felt the prenuptial agreement was not fair because it did not give her enough share of her husband's fortune. She thought she deserved one-half of Trump's wealth, and she was ready to go to court to fight for it.

With all his problems, it was the worst time in Donald Trump's life.[3] But the media attention he had always enjoyed kept right on going. Now, instead of flattering articles about his wealth and talent, the media rushed to print every possible detail they could get about his financial downfall and his marital problems.

His status as a public figure, which he had enjoyed for so long, was now working against him. Day by day, he had to endure public humiliation. And he knew lots of people were delighted to see him in trouble. He was also especially distressed by the upsetting effect all the media attention about his separation from Ivana was having on his children.

Nevertheless, Trump's "can-do" spirit, which had gotten him so far, would not fail him in his time of peril. Reflecting about that time in his life, he later wrote: "It never occurred to me to give up, to admit defeat."[4]

All these plans, however, would mean that the banks would not get back all the money they had loaned him. So why would they even think of agreeing to his pleas for

> **"It never occurred to me to give up, to admit defeat."**

A Bailout

Just as he had done with all of his property deals, he was ready to fight. Trump knew the first thing he needed to do was to gather his bankers together and try to work out arrangements with them. He needed them either to reduce his loan payments, or refinance his loans at lower interest rates so he would not have to pay so much money each month. Another option was to persuade them to postpone his payments for several years.

help? The reason is that if they did not, and Trump did, indeed, file for bankruptcy, the banks would only get his buildings, which they did not want, because they would have to sell them at huge losses. The banks would end up with some of their loaned money back, but not nearly as much as they would if they helped Trump, and he was able to get back on his feet financially.

So that is what many of them did. Trump called a meeting of representatives from ninety banks from around the world that had loaned him money. They met in his conference room at Trump Tower or attended by conference call. About that meeting, he would later write:

The Trumps wave to reporters as they board the *Trump Princess*. The vessel boasted eleven luxurious guest suites and living quarters for forty-eight crew members and servants. Trump used the yacht to entertain business clients and high-stakes Atlantic City gamblers.

"I will never forget the day I was forced to call the banks to renegotiate my loans. This was something that I never thought could happen to me."[5] Trump explained his situation to the bankers, asked for their help, and clearly pointed out the advantages for them if they helped him instead of cutting him loose. He later wrote about that meeting: "That was the biggest bet of my life, and boy, did it pay off!"[6]

Many banks agreed to work with him, easing his immediate debt by at least $65 million, and delaying payments on much of the rest. Some banks, on the other hand, refused to negotiate a deal with him. Trump would never forget or forgive the banks that chose not to help him.

Trump also fought back with the press, always appearing upbeat and proclaiming that his difficulties would work out over time. Looking back and trying to learn from his problems, Trump admitted, "I got caught up in the buying frenzy."[7] He also realized that he was "too competitive for [his] own good."[8]

> "I will never forget the day I was forced to call the banks to renegotiate my loans. This was something that I never thought could happen to me."

In the meantime, to get more cash Trump sold his most unprofitable holdings, including Trump Plaza of the Palm Beaches; his yacht, the *Trump Princess*; and his airline shuttle service. He also turned to his family for help. His father, Fred, helped him with a multimillion dollar loan. He also borrowed millions of dollars from his siblings. By the time Trump was through fighting for his business, he was still financially alive.

A Second Chance

Even so, he would have to continue to juggle funds carefully for the next several years to stay afloat. In 1990, Trump published his second book, *Trump: Surviving at the Top*, with the help of writer Charles Leerhsen. As with his first book, this one also became a *New York Times* best seller.

Trump's divorce from Ivana was granted in late 1990. She gave up her lawsuit and ended up settling for the terms in the prenuptial agreement. With that, in 1991, she received $10 million in cash, their Greenwich, Connecticut, home, $100,000 each year in child support for each of their three children, $350,000 each year for alimony, and a $4 million housing allowance. Despite their divorce, Trump continues to claim that he will always love Ivana.

Trump's relationship with Marla Maples moved forward. In October 1993, they had their first and only child together, a daughter whom they named Tiffany Ariana. Two months later they were married at the Plaza Hotel, with more than one thousand guests attending the ceremony.

Meanwhile, Trump had long been working on yet another new development. This would be at the West Side Rail Yard at Sixtieth Street along the Hudson River. It had long been one of the most valuable undeveloped pieces of property left in Manhattan. Trump had wanted to build on this property since his career in Manhattan began years earlier. But without city support, his development proposals fell flat, and he ended up letting his option on the property lapse. Nevertheless, he bought it back again in 1985, and he had been fighting with the city and community groups about plans for the property ever since.

In typical fashion, Trump planned for a massive development of the West Side Rail Yard. Along with up to seven thousand apartments in six seventy story buildings, he also wanted to include business offices and a big shopping mall on the property. On top of that, Trump wanted the area to include the world's tallest building. He was convinced that such a building should be in New York City, rather than in Chicago, where the Sears Tower claimed the title at that time.

Donald Trump married his second wife, Marla Maples, in 1993. Together they would have Trump's fourth child, Tiffany.

Trump also knew that the NBC television studios, located in New York City's Rockefeller Center, were considering moving to a less expensive location. He wanted to entice them to move to his West Side development. To encourage them, he planned to build television and movie studios as part of the complex. He wanted to call the development Television City.

Just as with his earlier attempts to develop the property, Trump ran into immediate opposition from the city, as well as from many of the homeowners in the surrounding neighborhoods. They formed a group called Westside Pride to work against him. They campaigned to the city officials that Trump's proposed project would be bad for the area. They complained that by adding so many new residents in the area, it would create massive traffic problems and overcrowded schools. They also didn't want high-rise apartment buildings there.[9]

After years of battle with the city and neighborhood opposition, all the affected groups finally came up with a

What's in a Name?

Trump Place was in the news again after the 2016 presidential election. Although the buildings in the Riverside South development are owned and managed by Chicago-based real estate group Equity Residential, the Trump name was featured prominently on their facades in large gold letters.

After Trump's contentious campaign and victory, he lost a vote of a different kind. Just days after he became president-elect, hundreds of residents of Trump Place petitioned to have the Trump name removed from their buildings.

The petition read, "Trump's appalling treatment of women, his history of racism, his attacks on immigrants, his mockery of the disabled, his tax avoidance, his outright lying—all are antithetical to the values we and our families believe in."

compromise plan. The development would not include the world's tallest building; nor would it be home to NBC, which remained at Rockefeller Center. Instead, the development, to be called Riverside South, would include fewer apartments than Trump had originally proposed. The final plan allowed for up to 5,700 units in 16 high-rise buildings. In addition, Riverside South would include a 23-acre (9 ha) public park along the Hudson River. The new plan was approved by the city in late 1992.

Trump later sold the land to a group of Hong Kong investors. Still, he maintained a high profile with the project, as the investors hired him to build and manage the development. Trump's name is prominently displayed on the buildings. Along with Riverside South, the project is often referred to as Trump Place. About the project, Trump later wrote: "Some things are worth waiting for . . . This could prove to be my finest contribution to the city of New York."[10]

Slowly, by the mid-1990s, Trump began to pull back from the brink of financial disaster. At the same time, the real-estate industry was beginning to come out of its slump. Trump would later write about his close call with financial ruin with the words, "My policy is to learn from the past, focus on the present, and dream about the future."[11]

Back to Business

● ●

By the mid-1990s the country's economy was improving, which served to help Trump's financial situation. The next ten years would bring many more changes to Donald Trump's busy life. In 1994 his father—long his business partner and advocate—died from pneumonia. Fred Trump had also suffered from Alzheimer's disease. He was ninety-three years old when he died. Despite his advanced age, Fred had never retired, each day going to his office on Avenue Z in the Bronx in a chauffeur-driven limousine. His wife, Mary, continued living in the Trump family home in Queens.

Donald had remained close to his father throughout his life. He would later write: "I learned to think like a billionaire by watching my father, Fred Trump. He was the greatest man I'll ever know, and the biggest influence on my life."[1] And Fred had always stood by his son, through good times and bad. Even during his son's most difficult financial times, Fred supported him, saying,

Donald Trump posed with his proud parents, Fred and Mary. Trump credited his father for teaching him to be successful in the real estate business.

· ·

"Don't worry about Donald, I've watched him all of his life. Donald is a winner and will have no troubles."[2]

Always Moving Forward

Despite his father's death, Trump moved his organization forward. In 1994, his next project took him to a building on the southwest corner of Central Park. Built in 1969, the outdated, fifty-two-story building was owned by the General Electric Investment Corporation. Trump wanted to buy it, gut it, and strip the building's exterior down to its steel frame. Then he would reconstruct it

81

into a building that would contain a combination of luxury hotel rooms and condominiums.

Construction began in 1995. When completed, the new structure contained 264 condominiums and 164 hotel suites. Trump also added a highly rated restaurant, called Jean-Georges, in the building. Trump called his newest creation the Trump International Hotel and Tower. Throughout his career, Trump always looked forward to his next project. In fact, he said he liked to have at least ten business deals going at the same time.[3] As he would write: "To be always moving toward a new goal . . . [is] as close to happiness as you're going to get in life."[4]

Even so, part of the Trump Organization was not always moving forward. By 1995, despite his earlier loan restructuring, Trump's Atlantic City hotel/casinos were still not making enough money to cover the loan payments he had to make on them. To get more cash, Trump pulled his Atlantic City properties together and formed a publicly held company called Trump Hotels and Casino Resorts. That meant that he could raise much-needed money by selling stock, or shares of ownership, in the newly formed company. The downside for Trump was that he would be responsible to his stockholders and a board of directors. They could

> "To be always moving toward a new goal . . . [is] as close to happiness as you're going to get in life."

vote to disapprove of his decisions and leadership. It put him in an uneasy position, which he was not used to and did not like.

Up until this time, as president and chief executive officer (CEO) of the Trump Organization, Trump was solely in charge of all his properties. And he liked it that way, because he made all the company decisions and was responsible for explaining them to no one but himself. Yet at this point, he saw the option of making his casinos a public company as a necessary evil.

In 1996, Trump turned his attention to an old, vacant office building at 40 Wall Street in Manhattan. With seventy stories, at the time it was built it had been second only to the Empire State Building in height. But over time, the once-grand office building in the heart of Manhattan's financial district had become rundown. Trump, however, recognized the value of the property, with its prime location and its spectacular views. He wanted to turn it back into a spectacular office building.

So he bought the building and gutted it from top to bottom. Then he rebuilt its interior into beautiful new offices. He also added an elegant lobby on the ground floor, spending an estimated $200 million on the project. When he was finished, he named the renovated building the Trump Building at 40 Wall Street. Always proud of his work, Trump considered it one of the best deals he ever made.

Trump had claimed for years that his name on a building added to its value. In one of his books he wrote: "Trump has become a great brand name, due to my rigorous standards of design and quality."[5] And his 40 Wall Street building would be no exception. Its offices were quickly rented, and the building became another big success for Trump. That same year, Trump partnered with CBS to own and broadcast the three largest beauty competitions in the world: Miss Universe, Miss USA, and Miss Teen USA. Later he changed networks, going with NBC instead, as CBS did not promote the pageants as aggressively as he wanted.

In 1997, Trump's third book, *Trump: The Art of the Comeback*, appeared in bookstores. Writer Kate Bohner helped him put the book together. It would be his third best seller. As for his very successful venture into the publishing world, Trump would write: "I like writing books, and if I like something, I can find the time for it!"[6]

Celebrity Status

By 2004, the Trump name was recognized throughout the United States. And in New York City, where he would often walk from Trump Tower to inspect his nearby properties, he was forced to hire a bodyguard to accompany him because of the stir his presence caused among people on the streets. Many wanted his autograph. Some just wanted to touch him, hoping his flair for making money would rub off on them

A New Love

Meanwhile, Trump and his second wife, Marla, had endured a stormy marriage. About the problems in their marriage, he later wrote: "Sadly . . . we just drifted apart. Our lifestyles became less and less compatible."[7] Still, she had stuck by him during his darkest years, when his business empire and marriage to Ivana were falling apart. But by 1997, the couple separated, finally divorcing in 1999. Trump gave her $1 million, along with generous ongoing child support for their daughter, Tiffany.

Around that time, Trump met the woman who became his new love interest—Melania Knauss. Born in Slovenia (then part of the former Soviet Republic of Yugoslavia), she was twenty-four years younger than him. A stunning brunette, she was modeling in the United States for a fashion event when they met. Their relationship took off from the start. Trump would later describe Melania as "just as beautiful on the inside as she is on the outside."[8] She also had a calming influence on his hectic life, and he felt lucky to be with her. Before long, she moved into Trump Tower with him.

The next year, Trump continued his successful run in the publishing world by writing his fourth book, *The America We Deserve*. He wrote it because he was concerned that America was seen as weak by other countries, such as Japan and Germany. Trump also candidly described what he saw as problems in the United States—government bureaucracy, the public-school system, and crime. According to one book description, "Throughout [the book] Trump points out problems and offers sensible, practical solutions."[9]

At the same time, Trump was considering the possibility of running for US president. Eventually, he decided against it, realizing that he was too outspoken to be successful in politics. And besides, he already loved the job he had.

"Play Golf"

Trump's next construction project would be known as Trump World Tower at United Nations Plaza. Located near the United Nations building on the East Side of Manhattan, with seventy stories, Trump claimed his new structure would be the world's tallest residential building.

As with all Trump's buildings, luxury was his first priority. It would contain one-, two-, and three-bedroom condominiums. It also offered four-bedroom penthouses, which included maid's quarters and wood-burning fireplaces, along with incredible views of the city. The building had a health club, a 60-foot (18 m) swimming pool, and a top-rated restaurant.

Over the next few years, along with constructing buildings, Trump turned his attention to his other passion—golf. He had begun playing when he was eighteen years old, and he considered it a great way to get business accomplished. He wrote: "Playing golf with a business associate . . . is seldom a waste of time."[10] In fact, in his book *Trump: The Art of the Comeback* he lists "Play Golf" as his number one comeback tip.

In 1999, Trump's first golf club opened in Florida. Located in West Palm Beach, it was called the Trump International Golf Club. As with his buildings, Trump planned to create the best golf course in the world. He spent $40 million creating a world-class, eighteen-hole golf course. The landscaping was spectacular, with tropical plants and trees, waterfalls, and meandering streams throughout. In addition, the course was graced with a magnificent Mediterranean-style clubhouse. Memberships at the exclusive golf club were set at $250,000. The next year, Trump's West Palm Beach Golf Club received a Five Star Diamond Award as the best golf course in Florida.

> **"Playing golf with a business associate . . . is seldom a waste of time."**

Trump would continue to expand his golf club holdings. One became the Trump National Golf Club, Westchester, located just thirty minutes from Manhattan. He also bought what would become the Trump National Golf Club, Bedminster, in Bedminster, New Jersey. It was already a world-class, eighteen-hole golf course on 525 acres (212 ha) of rolling New Jersey countryside. The clubhouse is an elegant, restored mansion built in 1939. Along with golf, the club also offers miles of horseback-riding trails, tennis courts, and several guest cottages.

In 2002, Trump bought the Ocean Trails Golf Course in Los Angeles, California. The 300-acre (121 ha) course extends along the Pacific coast, offering panoramic

An avid golfer, Donald Trump would renovate and develop many golf courses throughout his career. He considers golf a great way to conduct business.

ocean views from each of its eighteen holes. Trump renovated the course and upgraded it to his standards.

Also that year, Trump bought yet another building in Manhattan—the former Hotel Delmonico. Built in 1929, the property was located at Park Avenue and East Fifty-ninth Street. He turned it into thirty-five stories of luxury condominiums. The building was completed in 2004 and became known as Trump Park Avenue.

At the same time, Trump's casino properties were once again in financial trouble. They still were not making enough money to show a profit. Without that, Trump was unable to keep up with the maintenance they needed or to make improvements to be competitive with other Atlantic City casinos. So in October 2004, Trump faced his Atlantic City financial problems by restructuring his hotel/casino debt with the banks he owed money to, just as he had done years earlier.

Within a year, the company was on steadier footing financially, and it had pulled away from bankruptcy with a new name: Trump Entertainment Resorts Holdings. As part of that transaction, Trump gave up his title as chief executive officer, but remained the company's chairman of the board.

Still, after all he had accomplished, new adventures and even greater fame lay ahead for "the Donald."

Television
Celebrity

• • • • • • • • • • • • • •

I n 2002, television producer Mark Burnett would change Donald Trump's life with a simple telephone call. The two men had never met, but Burnett's fame in the television industry preceded him. Trump needed no introduction.

Burnett is a British-born entrepreneur who had made a huge name for himself in the United States as the creator of the popular reality competition show *Survivor.* He was calling Trump to see if he could film the final episode of *Survivor's* fifth season at Wollman Skating Rink in Central Park.

Trump agreed, and on the day the filming took place, he strolled over to make sure everything was going to Burnett's satisfaction. When he got there, he was astonished to see how the television crew had transformed the skating rink. They had made it look like a jungle to match Survivor's seasonal setting in Thailand. While there, he met Burnett, who asked to meet with Trump the following week.

The Start of Something Big

Survivor had first aired in the United States on CBS in 2000. Burnett got the idea for the show from a similar one that had become quite popular in England, and he had persuaded CBS to try an American version. On *Survivor*, which takes place in remote areas all over the world, contestants are divided into tribes. Each week they are pitted against each other to perform a variety of tasks, or "challenges."

Survivor would make television history. It became the first profitable and highly rated of what would become something new to television: the reality show. With its success, *Survivor* was quickly followed by many other reality shows such as *The Bachelor, American Idol*, and *Fear Factor*.

Many reality shows have failed to attract a large following and have been canceled after a short run. But popular or not, they are relatively inexpensive to produce. When a television network scores a hit reality show, it can be extremely profitable. Ever in search of a new idea for another hit reality show, Burnett met with Trump in New York to discuss his latest idea—a reality show based in the business world. Rather than set in a jungle like *Survivor*, Burnett's vision was for the new show to take place in the "concrete jungle" of New York City. He had read Trump's book *Trump: The Art of the Deal* years earlier when he was new to the United States and making a living selling T-shirts in California. He told Trump the book had changed his life. Now he wanted to work with Trump to try a reality show with a business theme. He thought the show would be "educational" for its viewers, later writing, "People would be able to see how the real business world works and what it takes to survive in it."[1]

At the same time, Jeff Zucker, president of NBC Entertainment, needed to find a replacement for the popular television show *Friends*. A long-running

Trump Reality

Although Zucker thought Burnett's concept with Trump had potential, there was some concern that people outside New York City would not find the show interesting. But Zucker remained positive, saying, "I knew that Donald was universal. He's been up, he's been down, he's been back up again."[2]

situation comedy, *Friends* would be ending a ten-year run on television, during which it had gained tens of millions of fans. With the show going off the air in 2004, it would leave a big hole in Thursday night television on NBC.

This was not the first time Trump had been approached about participating in reality television. But others' ideas had centered around filming his daily activities, and he was not interested. He said he could not do business with film cameras in his face all the time. But Burnett's idea was different: a thirteen-week job interview with Mr. Trump. The idea captured Trump's interest.

The Apprentice

With agreement on the show finalized between Trump, Burnett, and NBC, word was sent out to talent agents in major cities across the country to find applicants for the show. They advertised for "young business professionals looking to get a leg up in their careers."[3] Two hundred and fifteen thousand eager applicants responded. Each produced a ten-minute audition tape, along with a twelve-page application. That group was cut to eleven thousand, who were granted in-person interviews. The remaining fifty semifinalists were sent to Los Angeles to have a personal interview with Mark Burnett. He made the final selection of sixteen.

Why would these sixteen people be willing to take themselves out of their normal lives and away from their homes, families, and businesses for several months? Why would they agree to put themselves on a television show where they would be stressed, humiliated, and tested in front of millions of viewers? They were willing because the final winner would walk away with the opportunity to run one of Donald Trump's real estate projects for a year—with a salary of $250,000!

From the first, the participants were divided into two teams—eight men against eight women. The men called their team Versacorp; the women became the Protégé Corporation. In the weeks ahead, the teams would receive a new business assignment every two or three days. It might be selling lemonade to downtown New Yorkers or developing an advertising campaign for a hot new product. Another time, each team had to manage a restaurant for an evening. Over the entire first season, the teams would complete thirteen different business assignments.

On *The Apprentice*, Donald Trump presided over the show's contestants in his boardroom each season. Based on their performance of the business tasks they were assigned, Trump would decide who was fired and who was hired.

At the end of every task, each team's profits were counted. After all, making money is what business is all about. Whichever team had made the most money won. They were rewarded with a special treat, such as a fancy dinner at an exclusive New York City restaurant or the chance to meet a famous celebrity or sports star.

The losing team, on the other hand, had to pack their bags and face Donald Trump in his eerily dark, richly furnished boardroom. After a long session of grueling questions, finger-pointing, backstabbing, and excuses about why their team had lost, one contestant would see Trump's forefinger point at him or her and hear the dreaded words, "Your're fired!" At that point, the loser was left to slink off to a waiting cab, suitcase in hand, to be whisked to the airport and back home.

According to Bill Rancic, the final winner of *The Apprentice*, Season One, he had no idea what he was really getting into when Burnett picked him for the show. As he prepared for an uncertain amount of time filming in New York City, he later wrote that "it was tough for me to understand what was going on, or what I might or might not be getting myself into."[4] Yet he was willing to take the risk to get some "face time" with the man he considered to be the ultimate entrepreneur, Donald Trump.

Shooting for the first season took seven weeks. During that time, the contestants lived together in a luxurious eight-bedroom condominium in Trump Tower. Assisting Trump each week in deciding who would be fired were two of his top executives, George

H. Ross and Carolyn Kepcher. Once filming began, Trump was astonished with the amount of time it took from his already hectic schedule. Burnett had predicted it would cost Trump no more than three hours of his time each week. In reality, it took ten times that much. Nevertheless, Trump enjoyed working on the show. He especially loved the drama he added to the episodes when he entered the boardroom. And he had no lines to learn or acting to do. His job was to be himself, and the dialogue was completely unscripted.

Trump also enjoyed getting to know the show's job candidates, later writing: "The sixteen applicants quickly became people I liked and cared about . . . It wasn't easy to fire any of them."[5] On top of everything, Trump was delighted with the attention the show gave him and the Trump Organization. He saw it as free publicity and advertising.

> "The sixteen applicants quickly became people I liked and cared about. . . It wasn't easy to fire any of them."

The concept of a thirteen-week interview proved to make for very successful reality television. *The Apprentice* aired from January through April 2004. Trump took the title of executive producer for the show as well as host, and he was paid $50,000 per episode. NBC paid the season's winner their $250,000 salary when they went to work for Trump. During that first season an average of twenty million people watched each episode.

Only One Colorful Enough

Trump has made it clear that he thinks he was a big reason for the show's success. He does not hesitate to mention that a similar show with Martha Stewart only lasted one season. The reason? According to Trump, Stewart did not have the personality or charisma needed to keep viewers coming back. He would later say in an interview, "How do you think *The Apprentice* would have done if I wasn't a part of it? There are a lot of imitators now and we'll see how they'll do, but I think they'll crash and burn."[6]

On casting Trump, Burnett seemed to agree with his assessment, saying, "I knew clearly that there was only one master who was colorful enough, charismatic enough, who is really a billionaire, [that] was Trump."[7] And perhaps he was right.

> **I think that people learned that I'm a nicer person when I did *The Apprentice*.**

After the success of the first season, Trump negotiated with NBC for a higher salary for the second season. He used the *Friends* cast salaries to make his point in asking for $18 million per episode. He did not get that, but according to Trump, he got more than $1.25 million per episode.

Despite the first season's success of *The Apprentice*, fewer television viewers watched the show's second season. Some thought it was because the cast members were not as interesting and entertaining as they had been

Donald Trump has authored a number of books with the assistance of professional writers. Most became best sellers. Here, Trump autographs copies of his book *The America We Deserve*.

in the first season. Even so, the second season's finale drew an impressive sixteen million viewers.

At the same time, the show's episodes became part of business curriculum at some universities. Students would view them and discuss the business ethics and tactics used in each week's task. The show also had an effect on people's view of Trump. As he would admit, "I think that people learned that I'm a nicer person when I did *The Apprentice*."[8]

Back on Top

The year 2004 was an eventful one for Donald Trump. In addition to *The Apprentice* debut, he also released two more books. One was written with the help of Meredith McIver and called *Trump: How to Get Rich*. According to one review: "Trump's books have done an effective job of capturing his grand personality in print, and this volume is no exception."[9] Trump's other book that year was *Trump: The Way to the Top: The Best Business Advice I Ever Received*. It contains business advice he gathered from more than one hundred other successful business people.

The Apprentice successfully continued, with the sixth season taking place in Los Angeles, California, rather than New York City. For seasons five and six, Trump also used winning project managers, former *Apprentice* winners, his daughter Ivanka, and his son Donald Jr. as his advisers instead of George Ross and Carolyn Kepcher. Season seven aired in January 2008, this time with celebrities as candidates, called *Celebrity Apprentice*. The winner earned prize money for their favorite charity.

As winner of *The Apprentice*'s first season, Bill Rancic's prize was to help manage one of Trump's in-process projects: Trump International Hotel and Tower, Chicago. Located in downtown Chicago, Illinois, the massive building opened in 2008. With ninety-eight stories of high-end condominiums, along with luxury hotel guest rooms and suites, it became the fourth tallest building in the United States. The building also contains a health club and spa, exclusive retail shops, and fine restaurants. And according to Trump, it would hold the title as the world's tallest residential building. The cost for the building was estimated at more than $800 million.

By 2005, in addition to his golf courses and hotel/casinos, Trump had eleven buildings in Manhattan with his name on them. While some may criticize that as being egotistical, still, he insists it assures his clients of the high quality they can expect from him. And he has no intention of discontinuing the practice.

Expanding
the Empire

· · · · · · · · · · · · · · ·

Even though much of his time was taken up by the success of his television show, Donald Trump continued with his real estate ventures. He also would release more books, with *Trump: The Best Golf Advice I Ever Received* appearing in 2005.

At the same time, his family also expanded. Trump and his love of six years, Melania Knauss, were married on January 22, 2005. The couple had become engaged earlier, after he had given her a thirteen-carat diamond engagement ring costing an estimated $1.5 million. They were married in the Bethesda-by-the-Sea Episcopal Church in Palm Beach, Florida. About 450 guests, including a number of celebrities, attended.

In 2006, Trump's next book, *Why We Want You to be Rich: Two Men—One Message*, was published. He wrote it in partnership with another well-known entrepreneur, Robert T. Kiyosaki, along with Meredith McIver and Sharon Lechter. *Publisher's Weekly* reviewed the book, writing: "[T]his collaboration of real estate magnate and

Donald Trump poses for photographers with his family in Trump Tower after announcing his intention to run for president. Pictured with their own families are Eric Trump, Barron Trump, Melania Trump, Donald Trump Jr., Ivanka Trump, and Tiffany Trump.

• •

rags-to-riches financial guru manages to entertain and to inform."[1]

Also that year, Trump's first child with Melania, Barron William Trump, was born. Meanwhile, Trump's other children had grown up. All three of his children with Ivana went to work for the Trump Organization as vice presidents of real estate acquisition and development.

Continuing to Build—and Diversify

Donald Trump's life seemed to be exactly as he wanted it. And despite his ever-increasing number of projects, he showed no sign of slowing down. To the contrary, his real-estate projects only continued to mount. In the next years Trump turned his attention back to developing golf courses. He opened one in Colt's Neck, New Jersey, in 2008, and another in Washington, DC, in 2009. Those were followed in 2010 by clubs in Hudson Valley, New York, and in Philadelphia. Additional golf clubs and resorts in North Carolina, Florida, Scotland, Ireland, and Dubai would follow over the next years.

Trump did not stop with real estate projects. In addition to his television career and book collection, in 2005 he also established Trump University, later renamed the Trump Entrepreneur Initiative. It offered online and correspondence classes in such topics as marketing, real estate, and entrepreneurship. Because it was not an accredited university, it could not grant college credits or degrees. Still, it offered opportunities for rising business people to learn how to become more successful.

Trump University came under criticism by some of its students for not providing courses that were worth the cost of the classes. While Trump maintained that the overwhelming number of students were highly satisfied with the courses, still, several lawsuits against the university were filed. The university basically ceased operation in 2010.

Trading on his name's association with luxury and quality, Trump also developed a signature collection of Trump products, including Trump Steaks; the Trump Home Collection, which sells furniture, rugs, home-decorating items, and lighting fixtures; and the Donald J. Trump Collection of men's clothing and accessories. He also has a production company in Los Angeles, called

Trump International

In addition to his properties in New York, New Jersey, California, Illinois, and Florida, Donald Trump's name can be seen on hotels in Hawaii, Nevada, Washington, DC, and Virginia. He has also made his mark outside the United States, with hotels in the Dominican Republic, South Korea, Canada, Panama, Brazil, and Scotland. Most of these projects bear Trump's name, even though he does not own the properties himself. Other developers, recognizing the value of the Trump name, pay him to use it on their buildings

Trump Productions, and a real estate agency, Trump International Realty, which specializes in selling luxury properties.

Trump has always taken a lot of kidding about his hair. And he good-naturedly laughs right along. His hair got more attention than ever once he appeared on *The Apprentice*. But he likes his hair. He admits it might not be his strongest asset, but he has written: "I've been combing (my hair) this way for a long time and I might as well keep doing it."[2] He emphatically denies that he wears a wig, writing, "My hair is one hundred percent mine."[3]

Keys to His Success

Trump has established a reputation for hiring very capable women for high positions in the Trump Organization. He thinks that women work harder to prove themselves.[4] He explained his philosophy this way: "I'm not a crusader for feminism, I'm not against it, either. I'm just oblivious to a person's gender when it comes to hiring people and handing out assignments."[5]

At the same time, like his father Trump has no respect for weakness in people. He views weakness as the inability to stand up for yourself or to express an opinion with confidence. Rather, he thinks people should not be worried about offending others and should be ready to take on opposition directly. "Toughness is pride, drive, commitment, and the courage to follow through on things you believe in, even when they are under attack," he has written. "It is solving problems instead of letting them fester. It is being who you really are, even when society wants you to be somebody else."[6]

> "Toughness is pride, drive, commitment, and the courage to follow through on things you believe in, even when they are under attack. It is solving problems instead of letting them fester."

Trump is also well known for his germophobia; that is, a person with an unusually high fear of germs. He washes his hands frequently and is uncomfortable with the common business practice of shaking hands. As he said in an interview, "I think shaking hands is barbaric."[7] Rather, he prefers the Japanese practice of a simple short bow to greet others and show respect.

Donald Trump and his children are involved with several charities including the New York City Police Fund and the Police Athletic League, which develops and conducts programs to help children in New York City. The Eric Trump Foundation raises money to help children battling life-threatening diseases at St. Jude Children's Research Hospital. And Ivanka Trump works with an organization sponsored by the United Nations called Girl Up. It encourages American girls to promote and raise money to help adolescent girls in underdeveloped countries.

With all his projects and products, Trump's wealth and fame has continued to grow as well. He charges $250,000 to give a speech, and he had a star in his name added to the Hollywood Walk of Fame in front of the Kodak Theater in 2007. In late 2016, Forbes magazine estimated his wealth to be approximately $3.7 billion.

Conquering Politics

Trump entered the 2016 presidential race in 2015, and against all odds became the Republican nominee for president. He ran against Democratic nominee Hillary Rodham Clinton. Trump entered the campaign with no political experience; he had never campaigned for, or held, political office. In contrast, Clinton was a well-known political figure, having served the country as first lady, as US senator from New York, and as secretary of state under President Obama.

Campaigning was fierce between the two nominees. Both traveled across the country holding rallies to win supporters. Both ran television advertisements and organized volunteers to make telephone calls and knock on doors to encourage people to vote for their candidates. They also held three nationally televised debates to expose the American public to their political positions and vision for the country's future.

As a campaigner, Clinton held the advantage over Trump. She was used to the campaign process and how to get it organized and funded. Trump, on the other hand, was new to the process and not as well prepared. Still, Trump's rallies were often attended by thousands. Many voters were familiar with Clinton's views because of her long political life. But with Trump as a political newcomer, lots of potential voters wanted to find out what he stood for.

With the presidential campaign underway, polls were taken frequently, just as they had been during the primary season. They were a way to gauge the competition between Trump and Clinton and determine who might have the edge to win the election. As the campaign progressed, poll after poll seemed to favor Hillary Clinton. After all, Trump, with his political rhetoric, had offended several large groups of voters, including Latinos, women, the physically disabled, veterans, and Muslims. With so many unhappy with Trump, the general expectation as voting day approached was that Clinton would win the election.

Interest and anticipation were high as election day approached. On November 8, 2016, voters swarmed to their voting locations. In some areas voters waited in line for hours because of the large turnout. As the nation went to bed that night, a majority was confident that Clinton would become the country's new president.

But November 9 brought the unexpected. Just like a surprise ending in a movie, the country woke up to the news that Donald J. Trump was their president-elect. While Clinton had won the popular vote by over two million votes, Trump had won in states that brought him a majority of electoral votes.

The Electoral College

The number of electoral delegates each state is allotted is equal to each state's combined number of US representatives and senators. It is the electoral delegates who actually elect the president, based on the popular vote in their respective states.

In all states except Maine and Nebraska, each state's electoral delegates are awarded on a "winner takes all" basis, depending on the state's popular vote for president. This makes it possible for a presidential candidate to win the national popular vote, but lose the electoral vote if they win the popular vote in states with fewer electoral delegates.

On a tour of Washington as president-elect, Donald Trump speaks to reporters from the US Capitol. With him are his wife, Melania, and Speaker of the House of Representatives Paul Ryan.

• • • • • • • • • • • • • • • • • • • •

The country immediately erupted with emotion and shock. Trump supporters were exhilarated with the results, while Clinton supporters were outraged and dismayed. Many were frightened in anticipation of changes the Trump administration might bring to the country. Demonstrations protesting Trump's election were staged in a number of cities across the country for several days.

With his unexpected win, Donald J. Trump would become the forty-fifth president of the United States. And while he would be stepping into largely unknown territory because of his lack of political experience, he and his team began to prepare. More than anything, with the country so divided, Trump's top priority would be to find ways to reassure his opponents and to reunite the nation.

Throughout his life, Donald J. Trump has been criticized and made fun of, as well as praised and almost worshipped. Some see him as a cutthroat businessman who enjoys destroying his competition. Others see him as outrageous and bigger than life.

As one person put it, "Donald is a character, a genuine New York character."[8] But no matter the variety of opinions about the man, there is no denying that he has made, and will continue to make, his mark on American society.

> For me the American Dream is not just a dream; it's a reality. "

Regardless of what lies ahead for Donald Trump, he remains ever the optimist, writing, "With the parents I had and this country as my backbone, anything was possible. I operated on that premise of possibility, and I'm walking, talking proof of the American Dream. For me the American Dream is not just a dream; it's a reality."[9] And based on his past performance, he will continue to make his dreams come true.

Chronology

1946 Donald John Trump is born in Queens, New York, on June 14.

1964 Graduates from New York Military Academy.

1968 Graduates from the University of Pennsylvania Wharton School of Finance.

1971 Moves to studio apartment in Manhattan, New York.

1972 Finalizes first multimillion dollar real estate transaction with the sale of Swifton Village in Cincinnati, Ohio.

1974 Obtains the option to buy two rail yards in New York City; buys the Commodore Hotel.

1977 Marries Ivana Marie Zelnickova Winklmayr; first child, Donald John Trump Jr., is born.

1980 Completes the renovation of the Commodore Hotel, which is renamed the Grand Hyatt; begins construction on Trump Tower.

1981 Buys Trump Plaza in New York City; second child, Ivanka Marie, is born.

1982 Buys weekend estate in Greenwich, Connecticut.

1983 Completes construction on Trump Tower; buys USFL New Jersey Generals.

1984 Opens Harrah's at Trump Plaza casino/hotel in Atlantic City, New Jersey; third child, Eric, is born.

1985 Buys Mar-a-Lago estate in Palm Beach, Florida;

opens Trump Castle casino/hotel in Atlantic City, New Jersey; renovates the Barbizon Hotel and 100 Central Park South; buys Trump Plaza of the Palm Beaches.

1986 Renovates and reopens the Wollman Skating Rink in Central Park.

1987 Publishes *Trump: The Art of the Deal*, which becomes a *New York Times* best seller; buys yacht, the *Trump Princess*.

1988 Buys the Plaza Hotel in New York City.

1989 Buys fleet of Boeing 727 airplanes to form Trump Air shuttle service; helicopter crash kills three Trump casino executives.

1990 Opens the Trump Taj Mahal hotel and casino in Atlantic City, New Jersey; publishes second book, *Trump: Surviving at the Top*; divorces Ivana Trump.

1992 Gains approval for Riverside South development at West Side Rail Yard.

1993 Child with Marla Maples, Tiffany Ariana, is born; marries Marla Maples.

1995 Creates public company, Trump Hotels and Casino Resorts, for his hotel/casinos in Atlantic City.

1996 Renovates 40 Wall Street to become the Trump Building at 40 Wall Street; completes Trump International Hotel and Tower, Manhattan.

1997 Publishes third book, *Trump: The Art of the Comeback*.

1999 Divorces second wife, Marla Maples.

2000 Publishes fourth book, *The America We Deserve*.

2002 Renovates Hotel Delmonico to become Trump Park Avenue.

2004 The first season of *The Apprentice* airs on NBC television; publishes fifth book, *Trump: How to Get Rich*; sixth book, *Trump: The Way to the Top: The Best*

Business Advice I Ever Received; and seventh book, *Trump: Think Like a Billionaire: Everything You Need to Know About Success, Real Estate, and Life.*

2005 Marries third wife, Melania Knauss; Atlantic City hotel/casinos emerge from bankruptcy, creating Trump Entertainment Resorts Holdings; begins construction of Trump International Hotel and Tower in Chicago; publishes books *Trump: The Best Golf Advice I Ever Received.*

2006 Fifth child, Barron William, is born; publishes series of three books for Trump University; publishes *Why We Want You to be Rich: Two Men—One Message* with Robert T. Kiyosaki.

2007 Publishes two more books for Trump University; has star with his name installed on the Hollywood Walk of Fame at the Kodak Theater in Los Angeles, California.

2008 Publishes *Trump: Think Big: Make it Happen in Business and Life* and *Trump: Never Give Up.*

2010 Publishes *Think Like a Champion: An Informal Education in Business and Life.*

2011 Publishes *Midas Touch*, with Robert T. Kyosaki.

2012 Publishes *Trump: The Best Real Estate Advice I Ever Received.*

2015 Publishes *Time to Get Tough: Make America Great Again*; enters 2016 presidential race as Republican candidate.

2016 Publishes *Great Again: How to Fix Our Crippled America*; wins Republican nomination for US president; is elected president of the United States of America.

Chapter Notes

Chapter 1: Republican Roller Coaster

1. Michael Kranish and Marc Fisher, *Trump Revealed: An American Journey of Ambition, Ego, Money, and Power* (New York: Simon & Schuster, 2016), p. 292.

2. Marc Shapiro, *Trump This! The Life and Times of Donald Trump: An Unauthorized Biography* (Riverdale, New York: Riverdale Avenue Books, 2016), p. 123.

3. CNN Special Report, "All Business—The Essential Donald Trump," aired September 5, 2016.

4. Kranish and Fisher, p. 329.

Chapter 2: Born to Win

1. Donald J. Trump, with Tony Schwartz, *Trump: The Art of the Deal* (New York: Random House, 1987), pp. 47–48.

2. Ibid., p. 48.

3. Robert Slater, *No Such Thing as Over Exposure: Inside the Life and Celebrity of Donald Trump* (Upper Saddle, N.J.: Pearson Education, Inc., 2005), p. 44.

4. Michael D'Antonio, *Never Enough: Donald Trump and the Pursuit of Success* (New York: St. Martin's Press, 2015), p. 59.

5. Gwenda Blair, *Donald Trump: Master Apprentice* (New York: Simon & Schuster, 2005, p. 19.

6. Timothy L. O'Brien, *TrumpNation:The Art of Being The Donald* (New York: Warner Business Books, 2005), p. 49.

7. Trump, *Trump: The Art of the Deal*, p. 50.

Chapter 3: A Tough Competitor

1. E. D. Hill, *Going Places: How America's Best and Brightest Got Started Down the Road of Life* (New York: Regan Books, 2005), p. 289.

2. Donald J. Trump, with Tony Schwartz, *Trump: The Art of the Deal* (New York: Random House, 1987), p. 53.

3. Timothy L. O'Brien, *TrumpNation: The Art of Being The Donald* (New York: Warner Business Books, 2005), p. 49.

4. Michael D'Antonio, *Never Enough: Donald Trump and the Pursuit of Success* (New York: St. Martin's Press, 2015), p. 59.

5. Trump, p. 45.

6. Gwenda Blair, *Donald Trump: Master Apprentice* (New York: Simon & Schuster, 2005), p. 23.

7. Trump, p. 64.

8. Ibid., pp. 64–65.

9. Hill, p. 290.

10. Trump, p. 45.

Chapter 4: Making It Big

1. Donald J. Trump, with Tony Schwartz, *Trump: The Art of the Deal* (New York: Random House, 1987), p. 70.

2. Gwenda Blair, *Donald Trump: Master Apprentice* (New York: Simon & Schuster, 2005), p. 42.

3. Robert Slater, *No Such Thing as Over-Exposure: Inside the Life and Celebrity of Donald Trump* (Upper Saddle, N. J.: Pearson Education, Inc., 2005), p. 61.

4. Donald J. Trump, with Meredith McIver, *Trump: How to Get Rich* (New York: Random House, 2004), p. 13.

5. Harry Hurt III, *Lost Tycoon: The Many Lives of Donald J. Trump* (New York: W.W. Norton & Co., 1993), pp. 88–89.

6. Blair, p. 54.

7. Michael Kranish and Marc Fisher, *Trump Revealed: An American Journey of Ambition, Ego, Money, and Power* (New York: Simon & Schuster, 2016), pp. 82-83.

8. Blair, p. 67.

9. Ibid., p. 69.

10. Kranish and Fisher, p. 83.

11. Jerome Tuccille, *Trump* (New York: Jove Books, 1988), pp. 169–170.

Chapter 5: To the Top of the Tower

1. Donald J. Trump, with Kate Bohner, *Trump: The Art of the Comeback* (New York: Random House, 1997), p. 109.

2. Donald J. Trump, with Tony Schwartz, *Trump: The Art of the Deal* (New York: Random House, 1987), p. 32.

3. Ibid., p. 99.

4. William E. Geist, "The Expanding Empire of Donald Trump," *New York Times Magazine*, April 8, 1984, section 6, page 28, column 2.

5. Trump, *Trump: The Art of the Deal*, p. 110.

6. Ibid., p. 111.

7. Ada Louise Huxtable, "A New York Blockbuster of Superior Design," *New York Times*, July 1, 1979, p. D25.

8. Trump, *Trump: The Art of the Deal*, p.117.

9. Ibid., p. 8.

10. Ibid. p. 39.

11. Ibid., p. 40.

12. Gwenda Blair, *Donald Trump: Master Apprentice* (New York: Simon & Schuster, 2005), p. 60.

13. Ibid.

14. Trump, *Trump: The Art of the Deal*, p. 121.

15. Ibid., p. 30.

Chapter 6: Spreading the Wealth

1. William E. Geist, "The Expanding Empire of Donald Trump," *New York Times Magazine,* April 8, 1984, p. 28, http://select.nytimes.com (September 14, 2007).

2. Donald J. Trump, with Tony Schwartz, *Trump: The Art of the Deal* (New York: Random House, 1987), p. 9.

3. Ibid., pp. 388–389.

4. Geist.

5. Michael Kranish and Marc Fisher, *Trump Revealed: An American Journey of Ambition, Ego, Money, and Power* (New York: Simon & Schuster, 2016), pp. 82-83.

6. Donald J. Trump with Charles Leerhsen, *Trump: Surviving at the Top* (New York: Random House, 1990), p. 155.

7. Gwenda Blair, *Donald Trump: Master Apprentice* (New York: Simon & Schuster, 2005), p. 147.

8. William H. Meyers, "Stalking the Plaza," *New York Times*, September 25, 1988, p. 1, http://select. nytimes. com/search (October 23, 2007).

9. Trump, *Surviving at the Top*, p. 19.

Chapter 7: Running on Empty

1. Donald J. Trump, with Charles Leerhsen, *Trump: Surviving at the Top* (New York: Random House, 1990), pp. 166–167.

2. Robert Slater, *No Such Thing as Over-Exposure: Inside the Life and Celebrity of Donald Trump* (Upper Saddle, N. J.: Pearson Education, Inc., 2005), p. 102.

3. Donald J. Trump, with Kate Bohner, *Trump: The Art of the Comeback* (New York: Random House, 1997), p. 4.

4. Ibid., p. 3.

5. Ibid., p. 16.

6. Ibid., p. 17.

7. Trump, *Trump: Surviving at the Top*, p. 5.

8. Ibid.

9. Ibid., pp. 82–83.

10. Donald J. Trump, with Meredith McIver, *Trump: How to Get Rich* (New York: Random House, 2004), p. 43.

11. Trump, *Trump: The Art of the Comeback*, p. xix.

Chapter 8: Back to Business

1. Donald J. Trump, with Meredith McIver, *Trump: Think Like a Billionaire* (New York: Random House, 2004), p. xiv.

2. Donald J. Trump, with Kate Bohner, *Trump: The Art of the Comeback* (New York: Random House, 1997), p. 8.

3. Donald J. Trump, with Charles Leerhsen, *Trump: Surviving at the Top* (New York: Random House, 1990), p.120.

4. Ibid., pp. 12–13.

5. Donald J. Trump with Meredith McIver, *Trump: How to Get Rich* (New York: Random House, 2004), p. 51.

6. Trump, *Trump: Think Like a Billionaire*, p. 168.

7. Trump, *Trump: The Art of the Comeback*, p. 140.

8. Trump, *Trump: How to Get Rich*, p. 160.

9. Amazon.com, *The America We Deserve*, book description.

10. Trump, *Trump: Surviving at the Top*, p. 64.

Chapter 9: Television Celebrity

1. Donald J. Trump, with Meredith McIver, *Trump: How to Get Rich* (New York: Random House, 2004), p. 214.

2. Timothy L. O'Brien, *TrumpNation: The Art of Being The Donald* (New York: Warner Business Books, 2005), p. 16.

3. Bill Rancic, *You're Hired: How to Succeed in Business and Life* (New York: Harper Business, 2004), p. 143.

4. Ibid., p. 148.

5. Trump, p. 220.

6. Timothy L. O'Brien and Eric Dash, "The Midas Touch, With Spin on It," *New York Times*, September 8, 2004, http://select.nytimes.com (October 23, 2007).

7. "Mark Burnett on *The Apprentice*," Disc 5: Bonus Features, *The Apprentice, The Complete First Season*, DVD (Universal City, Calif.: Universal Studios, 2004).

8. "The Boss: Donald Trump on *The Apprentice*," Disc 5: Bonus Features, *The Apprentice, The Complete First Season*, DVD (Universal City, Calif.: Universal Studios, 2004).

9. Amazon.com, *Trump: How to Get Rich*, Publisher's Weekly review.

Chapter 10: Expanding the Empire

1. Amazon.com, *Why We Want You to be Rich: Two Men—One Message, Publisher's Weekly* review.

2. Donald J. Trump with Meredith McIver, *Trump: How to Get Rich* (New York: Random House, 2004), p. 151.

3. Ibid.

4. Gwenda Blair, *Donald Trump: Master Apprentice* (New York: Simon & Schuster, 2005), p. 116.

5. Donald J. Trump, with Charles Leerhsen, *Trump: Surviving at the Top* (New York: Random House, 1990), p. 84.

6. Ibid., p. 228.

7. Rick Marin, "Hug-Hug, Kiss-Kiss: It's a Jungle Out There," *New York Times*, September 19, 1999, http://select.nytimes.com (October 23, 2007).

8. Timothy L. O'Brien, *TrumpNation: The Art of Being The Donald* (New York: Warner Business Books, 2005), p. 156.

9. Donald J. Trump, with Meredith McIver, *Trump: Think Like a Billionaire* (New York: Random House, 2004), p. 135.

Glossary

atrium An open hotel lobby with a very high ceiling.

bas relief A wall image slightly raised from the surface to give a three-dimensional effect.

borough A section of New York City.

cadet A student at a military academy.

commissioner A city official responsible for some aspect of the city's care or government.

condominium Multiple homes connected to each other, sometimes contained within a building.

deferment Excused from serving in the military for medical reasons.

elite Upper class.

germophobia A higher-than-normal fear of germs.

negotiate To bargain with another to make a deal.

opulent Luxurious.

penthouse Luxurious living quarters at or near the top story of a tall building.

political primary The state by state election of Republican and Democratic candidates for the US presidency.

quarrying Mining.

renovate To update or change.

siblings A person's sisters and brothers.

tax abatement Tax relief; excused from paying taxes for a period of time.

tenant One who rents an apartment, office, or house.

variance An exception to a standard procedure.

Further Reading

Books

D'Antonio, Michael. *Never Enough: Donald Trump and the Pursuit of Success.* New York, NY: Thomas Dunne Books, St. Martin Press, 2015.

Shapiro, Marc. *Trump This! The Life and Times of Donald Trump: an Unauthorized Biography.* New York, NY: Riverdale Avenue Books, 2016.

Southerland, Benjamin. *Donald Trump: A Biography of the Mogul Turned Presidential Candidate.* Lexington, KY: CreateSpace Independent Publishing Platform, 2015.

Story, H. *The Platform of Donald Trump Candidate for President of the United States.* Amazon Digital Services, 2015.

Websites

The Trump Organization
www.trump.com
The official website of the Trump organization's branches.

The White House
www.whitehouse.gov
The official website of the white house and president of the United States.

Index